Thirteen Broken Biscuits

Stay strong, stay positive,
never stop believing and never give up.

Alan Peter Whittaker

© Alan Peter Whittaker 2021

Alan Peter Whittaker has asserted his right under the Copyright, Designs and Patent Act, 1988 to be identified as the author of this work.

All rights reserved.

Contents

Prologue 1

Chapter One Childhood 5

Chapter Two Adolescence: 'Peanut Factory' National Sea Training College 40

Chapter Three My First Ship – M V Manchester Port 47

Chapter Four 1982: The Offshore Industry - Biggest Mistake of My Life 132

Chapter Five Driving Instructor 170

Chapter Six Captain Cargo – The Franchise 190

Chapter Seven The Big Family Fallout 209

Chapter Eight We Are All Equal 218

Acknowledgements 249

References 250

Prologue

'The belief that every man's experience ought to be worth something to the community from which he grew up in, no matter what that experience may be, so long as it was gleaned along the line of some decent, honest work, made me the writer that I am today. ... I overcame poverty, and lack of education, but I grew up to be much better for those hard times.'
Riis 1890.

The incidents in this book represent key occurrences and events in a life I view very much as a tale of two halves: 'child Alan' and 'adult Alan'. One half will show the reader what is was like to be born into poverty, the second how 'adult Alan' fought to overcome these handicaps to turn them into positives without looking back with any anger or resentment.

I embarked on a Creative Writing Master's degree as an individual who had little experience of formal writing practices, along with being diagnosed with severe dyslexia, but also it was important to me that my life story to date should encourage and inspire young, disadvantaged people to realise that no matter how difficult life is, obstacles can be overcome.

Writing an autobiography required a degree of research, both regarding the mechanics of writing, but also the tone it should take. My research uncovered the German concept of the 'Bildungsroman' or 'coming of age' novel, which is:

...a story of the growing up of a sensitive person, who looks for answers to his questions through different experiences. Generally, such a novel starts with a loss or a tragedy that disturbs the main character emotionally. He or she leaves on a journey to fill that vacuum. Literary Devices, 018

Another writer who overcame extreme poverty and became a successful writer is Catherine Cookson. Her autobiography *Plainer Still* (1995), reveals that like me, she had little formal education and overcame sickness, poverty and being raised in a difficult environment, similar to mine. Cookson has a unique 'voice', telling it how it was and how her own life's difficulties and setbacks through illness and the loss of her sight did not deter her from embarking on a writing career. Each stage of her life was a challenge and everything had to be worked for - again, just like myself. Despite this, the tone of her autobiography is uplifting and has a played a major part in my own ambitions to become a successful writer. Reading her autobiography inspired me to write my own.

Another inspirational work sited nearer to my own childhood home is Robert Roberts' *A Ragged Schooling: Growing up in the Classic Slum* (1971). I did not grow up in a 'slum' as such, but it was still very difficult, being one of eleven children. Roberts too overcame the hard times that he grew up in. Crucially his book showed me that tragedy can be leavened by humour. This is also apparent in Frank McCourt's *Angela's Ashes* (1996). Again, this is a narrator who has overcome a grindingly poor childhood that must have been difficult. However, black humour overrides this, such as when McCourt's father comes rolling out of the pub, blind drunk and sick, then when he finally makes it home, looks for sympathy, but does not get any. My own childhood, however, did not seem so funny at the time. But looking back now I can see how much humour there actually was in our household. I did not want my story to fall into the genre of 'misery memoir'. I wanted my readers to not only read about the sad times but to also enjoy the humour of the Whittaker family's struggle through life, and to see that they overcome all their hardships. The often dark humour should serve to offset what is quite poignant and sad. Another reason to use humour is that it was my intention to aim this story not only at the older generation but also at a younger audience and I wanted the story to be inspirational. I did not want to frighten them away with nothing but negativity and hardship.

Severe dyslexia, only diagnosed as an adult, has been a major issue for me throughout my life. The anxiety and turmoil it created has not prevented me from chasing my dream to be a writer and also a better person overall. In retrospect, I realise how my memory issues affected my learning at school, compounded by the fact there was no support available, i.e. study coaches, social services or extra tuition from the school education departments, at that time. I did find ways of overcoming any emotional anxieties by being loyal to my mam in helping her to feed my family. Through this I could face the challenges of overcoming setbacks to help me with my life's journey and to develop into the person that I have become today.

Dyslexia creates challenges in retaining information and also with writing and structuring work logically – obviously a potential problem when creating a long autobiography. After researching reading and writing strategies for dyslexic learners, I was able to understand the concepts of writing in stages. With determination and the will to succeed in achieving my true potential I feel that I have overcome any anxieties and obstacles that have stood in my way. This is what I have intended to portray in my work and to show other people with similar learning difficulties that anything is possible if they work hard enough.

I had to carry out historical research from scratch as there was little family material in the form of letters, photos, and newspaper cuttings, which would have proved useful. Information was sourced through archives from my childhood and relevant local history materials. A University of Salford librarian provided invaluable help in assisting me in mastering the digital sources and in 'filling the blanks' regarding my time at the Blackburn Convalescent Home as a child. One book in particular, Peter Higginbottom's *Children's Homes: a history of institutional care for Britain's young* (2017) provided essential background data. It offered additional links to institutions such as the website *childrenshomes.org.uk* which led to my being able to contact the local Children and Family Directorate for additional information about the convalescent home.

Lastly, I have to thank the following people for their ongoing and valuable advice and support in what has been a long and interesting quest. June Smith, senior librarian at University of Salford; my course tutors, Ursula Hurley and Scott Thurston, for their invaluable help and motivating me through challenging times. Most of all I must thank Anne Fernie, my study coach, who has been my rock. Most of what I have written has only been possible with her help and guidance. There is still much to do in continuing my photojournalism and travelling to developing countries in order to highlight the plight and hardship that so many children have to try and overcome. But when I started this story it was my intention to have it published and promoted to people like myself in the hope that it will inspire them to achieve whatever they set their heart on.

CHAPTER ONE

CHILDHOOD

Mam always told me that I would have to sleep four-in-a-bed, when I was old enough to understand how poor we were. I was never sure from one night to another which or whose bed I was sleeping in, but it didn't seem to make any difference because the mattress and bedding was always wet from my brothers and sisters pissing the bed every night.

I grew up as the fourth child in a family of thirteen. The eldest was Maureen but as she was not my father's daughter, she never lived with us. Next in order of age came David, Arthur, me, Linda, Michael, Susan, Patricia, Carol and Beverley. We also had another sister Karen who we never saw as she was put up for adoption a few days after her birth. I was the only one with a second name -'Peter' - and to this day I have no idea why. We joked in the family that our parents must have planned to have another son after Michael, but they didn't so they used the 'leftover' name for me. We were well known in the area but not in a good way. We were the 'Whittaker tribe' and poor with it. Everyone knew and not everybody liked it. We lived in a three-bedroomed council house in Baguley, Wythenshawe, South Manchester, which was built as a 'garden city' in the 1920s to house inner city Mancunians away from the dirt and grime of Manchester.

Wartime building restrictions were lifted in the late 1940s and by the 1950s it was the biggest council estate in Europe.

While studying for my photography degree, I came across the work of Shirley Baker photographer.

> 'Shirley's photographs have been described as a grim record of inner-city poverty. However, in these her images one also finds humor, formalist and aesthetic expectation, as well as her concern for narrative drama. Her subject matter, most commonly women and children, with men less frequently observed, expresses her curiosity for children's play and women's daily lives, and human interaction and communication.'
> 'The Street Photographs' by Shirley Baker https://shirleybakerphotography.com/the-street-photographs/

No.9 Bowland Rd, Baguley, Wythenshawe, Manchester, where I grew up with my parents and brothers and sisters. The front of the house in this image has been modernised. It didn't look like this when I was a child living there.

It sounds good but it wasn't really for a family as big as ours. We were squashed in, four and five to a bed: not a happy experience if the bed was wetted. When it was time to go upstairs to bed, we would grab coats from the downstairs bannister as these were our 'blankets' for the night. Furious fights would break out for the limited supply. The bed springs would creak and the flocks and feathers used to fill cheap mattress would fly as the siblings launched and hurled themselves at each other furiously.

My father worked in a steel mill for twelve hours a day. He couldn't have had much of a life - the same thing day in, day out. He was a well-built man, strong as an ox. About six feet with little hair; this could have been because of all the worries he must have had trying to raise us all on a poor man's wage. There wasn't any such thing as holidays or trips out. I don't ever recall seeing him and my mam out together. He died at forty-five (I was thirteen years old), leaving my mother (who was not in the best of health) to cope alone with all her children. The youngest child, Beverley, was not in good health either. In 1968, aged seven, she died of a hole in the heart.

Sunday morning in our household was bath day. This, however, was a daunting experience for me as it would take place in our kitchen at the back of the house. My dad sat me on top of the kitchen sink with my feet immersed in water. The bottom half of my body was washed with carbolic soap. 'Stand up!' he would snarl as he washed the remainder of my filthy body, 'you're not going out to play until I've scrubbed you down with this soap!' I would wriggle in protest, causing him to threaten me, 'Either you keep still, or I will hold you down while I scrape the dirt off you!'

My Mother

It was like a Dickensian scene. Unfortunately, we didn't have any money for curtains to cover the kitchen window, and this, of course, would be the time when my friends Norman and 'Dirty Barry' would come around the back and knock on the door to see if I was playing out. They had to pass the window and view me fully exposed to the entire world 'in all my glory'. I could hear them laughing and ducking up and down underneath the window; one of them gobbed on the glass, it ran down the window pane like a broken egg yolk.

'Ask your daddy to wash this off the window once he's washed your arse!' Dirty Barry mocked. 'Hey, guess what. I called round to Whittie's house this morning. He was stood on the sink stark naked; his dad bathed him with a big, horrid block of soap, which looked like a brick. Ha, ha, hey Whittie, did your daddy wash your bum and bollocks? Looks like he missed a bit, your neck's filthy, ha, ha,' Dirty Barry guffawed. 'Ha, ha. Yeah, Whittie, just like Miss at school when she dragged you up in front of the class and sneered, we have a 'Billy Bunter' in our classroom, what do we all think of that?'

They all joined in with the banter. Norman taunted, 'Hey, Dirty Barry, has your friend Whittie here been round to your house? It sure looks like it; you must have had a wash in the same filthy water as him, ha, ha!'

'Hey Norman, you're a wanker. What about you? With your ugly spotty face and scabby bony white knees, you prick.'

'According to our teacher we are all wankers, ha, ha.'

It provided plenty for them to laugh at.

In those days, the late 1950s to early 1960s, there wasn't much in the way of expensive toys for us to play with. But there was no shortage of green open spaces to play on and get up to mischief in Wythenshawe, especially near Baguley Hospital where we used to climb up the drainpipes to peep into the ward windows, only to be chased away by the angry porters. Most of the time, my short-ragged pants would end up hanging around my arse for all to see.

We made use of the outside, which became our playground: climbing trees, stealing apples and pears, which contributed to our food source. We did have an ancient, massive black and white T.V. It was the size of a washing machine, supported by four chunky wooden legs, this was coin-operated by a tanner (six old pennies, around three pence today) this was to help pay for the weekly rental from the supplier. However, as money was in short supply, we never seemed to have the pleasure of watching a programme to the very end because either the tanner would run out, or the electricity meter would need feeding. Apart from the meter having to be fed, the TV was always breaking down and it would be weeks before the repair man came to fix it.

So, in the absence of indoor entertainment, we amused ourselves by upsetting our neighbours: knocking on their door and hiding at the side of their houses. When they appeared at the door to see who was there, we whistled, but they couldn't see us. This would really piss them off, then we would knock again until they decided to chase us, but luckily, they could never catch up with us.

This is the entry/ginnel dividing our house from next door where we used to light bangers because the sound was *very* loud and echoed. My house is on the right-hand side leading to our back garden.

Sunday lunch was our main meal of the week, and was cooked on the open fire. As the saying goes, 'first up best dressed' and for this event, it was 'first in best fed'. I was at that age where if I was playing out, I lost track of time and arrived late for Sunday dinner. There weren't enough plates, knives and forks for us all to eat at one sitting. Since this was the main meal of the week, we were all very, very hungry, but my younger sister Linda would purposely hold back and take her time whilst eating her dinner to tease and torment me. She would even ask my mam if there were any 'seconds', even if she didn't really want any, just to see me wait as long as possible for my turn to eat. We never had any tables or chairs on which to sit and eat; we would just huddle around the fire with its black smoke seeping and smouldering from the wet coals that I had requisitioned from the railway lines. We would make loud slurping noises while we were eating just to annoy my mam and dad. Sometimes this would create a happy atmosphere in the room. If there were any leftovers after we had cleaned our plates (which wasn't very often), I would lick my plate clean and receive a slap over my head from my mam for my uncouth manners!

The local grocer shop ('The Meadow') was just up the road from where we lived, and they would sometimes sell me a bag of broken biscuits for thruppence (one-and-a- half new pence). This largesse was only available if there were any broken ones in the boxes. In eager anticipation, I would peep through the shop window to monitor the queue of customers waiting their turn to pay at the counter. When the queue backed onto the shelves at the far end where the biscuit boxes were located, I would stand with my hands behind my back, gently put my filthy mitts in the biscuit tins, and dig my claws into the heaps of goodies to break them up into small pieces. I had to be crafty not to alert anybody as I did my best to try and pick the tasty ones: chocolate and custard creams being the best. But I had to time my antics to fit in with when the women in the queue were gossiping (which wasn't very long) so as not to arouse any suspicion of the biscuits snapping. When I got to the front of the queue, I would ask them whether they had any broken biscuits for sale, knowing full well that they had.

Broken biscuit box

I was just dropping off to sleep one night, when I remembered that I had been eating some broken biscuits that I had hidden inside my coat pocket. I was so hungry that I looked inside of the torn lining in my filthy wet coat and found some crumbs that were wedged inside the pockets, so I scraped them up with my finger nails and sucked on my freezing chocolate mitts then I fell asleep.

There wasn't any decent furniture in our house. However, for some unknown reason which I never understood, my dad purchased a huge industrial-like fridge that occupied a full third of our tiny kitchen. The fridge was operated by a massive motor at the back, which sounded like a rumbling volcano. I had to use all of my skinny seven stone to pull on the massive handle on the huge vault-like door. Its interior light illuminated all the kitchen and hallway as well, with more brilliance than the kitchen's naked lightbulb. But it was empty inside. It was lit up like Blackpool illuminations, not that I had the luxury of going to Blackpool, I'd just heard about it from the well-off kids. There wasn't even any foodstuff in the pantry, let alone luxury items such as fresh fruit or meat.

In winter, the ice formed on the inside of our windows instead of the outside. Our 'bog' which was *indoors* was so tiny there wasn't enough room to swing a cat. There was no such thing as soft toilet paper, so we had to use the newspapers that I brought home from my paper round, which were torn into various sizes for use. My concerns were if I undressed in the school changing room for PE then yesterday's news could have been read from my arse! The method of using newspaper and old torn catalogue pages was common in the early 1950s and 1960s. Toilet rolls were a luxury we couldn't afford. Ours would be located on top of the toilet cistern and on many occasions, my mother would have to go fishing by putting her hands into the toilet bowl to release the sodden paper just to unblock it. Sometimes if she didn't perform this distasteful task, the remnants from everybody's *derriere* would float to the surface and spill over onto the floor. Not far from where we lived in Baguley there were some very old houses pre-war. They had no plumbing for a toilet which was situated outside (an outhouse) so they couldn't be flushed. They were emptied by the local council men who would remove the bucket from underneath the toilet and empty its smelly contents into big tanks on the wagon.

We were always short of wood to put on the fire in the front room, which was our only source of heat for the whole house. I used to walk along a train track and pick up pieces of coal from passing trains. Another fuel source was breaking down the fence that separated our gardens, but this did not go down too well with the next-door neighbours! Neither did the soot from our blocked chimney when it rained down onto their whites on the washing line, with the remainder landing on their cabbage patch. This regular occurrence would send Mrs Peters (not her real name) round to our front door shouting abuse through the letterbox, but we just laughed until she gave up and went back in.

One other source of heating was the little electric fire that also doubled up as a toaster. It had two elements: each barely provided the same warmth as a couple of candles. We used to hold a piece of bread against the elements, but it would stick and catch fire leaving the remnants of bread sticking to the fire and smelling. My eldest brother David would then practice his DIY skills by soldering the wires of the elements back together so that we could still use the fire for heating.

Most of the time, we couldn't afford to put money in our gas meter. One of the ways we would overcome this was to use foreign coins that were about the size of a shilling (five pence) that we would collect from kids in the school playground. Failing that, my brother David would find ways of breaking into the meter to access the shillings and foreign coins that were already in there, which we would then recycle back into the meter. Unfortunately, when the man came to read and empty the meter, there was never enough money to pay our quarterly gas bill. This then was entered into a book to be carried over to the next reading. However, it was the same every time he came to empty and read the meter.

Gas Meter

Friday was rent day when the rent man called round from the council to collect the weekly payment. However, we could never pay him, and my mother would say to me, 'Go to the front door when he knocks and tell him I'm not home'.

It was also the day my mother would keep me off school again to deal with the rent man who would use his fist to bang, bang, bang on the door.

'Tell him I'm not in, go on tell him I'm not in.'

'But, Mam, we can't keep doing this,' I gasped.

'Do you as you're told - shhh he will hear us, go on, go on and answer the door and tell him I'm not in!'

But I knew he could hear us, I was frightened to open the door, so I peered through the letterbox. I could see him standing there in his big black coat with his rent book in hand. He loomed threateningly, blocking out my view of the garden ... all I could see was a stained gabardine mac.

'My mam's not in!' I quavered.

He bent down and stared at me with his big dark eyes.

'My mammmmm isn't in!' I froze. I couldn't move, but my teeth were chattering, and I was sweating. I knew he could hear us both; the panic rose in my throat, and my voice squeaked. I could hear him breathing heavily behind the door. He was coughing and sputtering his words out.

'This being the same procedure every week - I will be back shortly!' he shouted.

We crouched, frozen, listening intently as the heavy steps clumped away and only breathed again as the gate clicked. Had he really gone? Would he be coming back? Shortly after, my mam received a letter stating that she had to report to the local payment office. However, as she never ventured out of the house, this was another task that was allocated to me, with a note saying that we could not pay 'this time'.

A mystery that remains to this day is why my mam never left the house. My friends used to tease me because they had never seen my mam outside of the house when other boys' mams were always shopping or doing the garden. They even made sarcastic remarks, suggesting that my dad kept her locked up somewhere inside. This made me angry because it wasn't true; she was always cooking and cleaning, leaving no time to do anything else. One of my mates said that he would knock on our front door until my mam opened it, but I punched him in the face and the next day he had a big shiner of a black eye. That's why we kids had to do all the shopping because she never had the time. Nevertheless, in hindsight, she also knew that we could steal a few groceries and get away with it. Many years later, especially when I was away at sea on lonely dark nights whilst on lookout, my mind would play tricks on me while I stared into the dark misty horizon. My eyes would water with the cold winds of the North Atlantic. Why didn't she ever go out? Was she really afraid of what the neighbours would say, sneering at her in her one and only torn coat, wearing her all-year-round black fur boots with holes in the stocking? She had varicose veins, they were popping out of her stockings like firecrackers. I wonder even today whether my mam and dad had any kind of a life. On reflection, her reluctance to go out was a combination of her domestic life but also her embarrassment and shame in front of the neighbours, who all looked down on her for having so many children and so little money.

My brother Arthur and I would always hang out together and even though he was four years my senior, he always seemed to end up in some kind of trouble. Nevertheless, as a 'littlun', I latched onto him while he would walk in front of me; I was always there in his wake. On one occasion, when I was about five years old, we were playing on a local building site where there were some flats being built. In those days, there was always a night watchman ('the Nicky') looking after the building and tools.

I can only remember fragments of what happened on that occasion, but we must have been playing around the fire that the

'Nicky' had made to keep warm throughout the night. Yet, I do recall that he had a petrol can located near his fire. I'm still unsure to this day what happened exactly, but somebody must have been spreading petrol onto the fire whilst I was within the vicinity of the flames. This resulted in the fuel splashing onto the left side of my body, which also caught fire. I am told that I was in considerable pain, and most of the left side of my face and my left arm were severely burnt. I was taken to our local doctor's practice, which was just down the road from where we lived. I do remember spending some time in the children's ward of Manchester's Booth Hall Hospital so this must have been a difficult and traumatic time for my parents. I can't recall how long I was in this hospital, but even today, some of the physical scars are still visible.

I was awarded around £1,000 as compensation through the courts, which in those days was regarded as a considerable amount of money. The funds were put in trust for me for when I reached 18 years of age, so I could use it to help me in my later years. Nevertheless, my parents approached the trust and asked them whether they would be willing to make an early supplementary payment so that they could purchase a new bicycle for me. They agreed to make a small additional payment to purchase the bike. I remember it being a blue cycle with chrome handlebars. At that point, I had never been on a bike, and I couldn't ride one. The task of teaching me how to ride a bike was given to my two older brothers David and Arthur. This was a frightening experience for me, and it didn't go down too well with the rest of my brothers and sisters because I had this new bike, and they had nothing, so jealousy was rife. I could see this in the way they were teaching me to ride the cycle. They had no patience with me and they were angry. On one occasion, I was doing really well riding in a straight line, but when I arrived at our gateway entrance, I had difficulty trying to turn the handlebars as I reached the entrance to the house. I went flying head first over the handlebars because I had only applied the front brake, which meant the bike and I crashed into our next-door neighbour's front hedge, sending the leaves of their bushes scattering in all directions. I still couldn't get the hang of it three months down the line. My constant crashing, due to me not being able to turn properly and flying over the bars, had by now created a huge hole in the hedge, which I used as a 'brake' (which may still be there today!). Still, I persevered until I was able to ride my brand-new bike with confidence.

One benefit of my hard-earned cycling skills was that I was able to get a part-time job as a paperboy at the local newsagents. We delivered papers to the neighbourhood and beyond. However, the favourite paper round was delivering down the country lanes, nicknamed 'The Lanes'. The reason for this is because there was a way in which I could 'cook the books' (so to speak). As well as delivering the papers on a Saturday morning, I had to revisit the customers and collect the weekly payments for the deliveries. I was given a small notebook with the customers' names and payments that were due, so when I received the cash from a punter, I would note it in the book as 'not paid', i.e. 'nil,' then I would keep the money, which was usually around 10 bob (50p). At the end of the day, I returned to the newsagents, handed over the book and some cash payments, so it wasn't too obvious. The newsagent took the money and the book from me and just put it to one side until the next week when I was handed the payment book again, and so it went on. I would just use a rubber to rub the 'nil' payments out (because I only used a pencil in this book), then I would adjust this to 'paid in full' from the last payment. The newsagent was none the wiser, so not only did I get paid for doing this job, but I also held onto some of the payments from customers.

It was a bit like Robin Hood robbing the rich to feed the poor, who were my family and me. The customers never lost anything by using this method, so understandably the 'lanes round' was in high demand from the other paper lads.

Apart from the paper round, I had two other part-time jobs. One of them was working Sundays on a market garden ('garden centre' today) This was backbreaking work for a thirteen-year-old. Part of my job was to drop small plants along a piece of string that stretched forevermore while the farmer worked next to me digging in the plants. On some occasions, we had to transfer manure from one plot to another, and we did this by using a trailer and towing it by tractor to another plot of land. But, once the top layer of the crust of the manure pile was removed, the smell was unbearable, like a broken sewer pipe. I was always sick at this point, and even to this day, when I smell something similar it takes me back. For all this sacrifice, my wage was about twelve shillings (60p) for a full day's work.

My third job was working as a van boy when I was still around thirteen, delivering bread from the local bakery. For this day's labour, I received around 10 shillings (a 'ten bob' note or 50p). However, this gave me an opportunity to steal some stale bread and cakes from the pigpen (a wire cage where stale baked goods were thrown and stored). The local farmer picked up these unwanted leftovers, took them to his farm and fed them to the pigs.

This was the owner's bungalow where I worked on the market garden. Now derelict and soon to be demolished, I used to sit on the front garden eating posh cakes and biscuits (whole ones not broken).

Feeding food scraps to pigs/'pig bins' was outlawed across the EU in 2002 after the BSE crisis in 1996 and the Foot and Mouth outbreak in 2001. In those days, there was no such thing as a sell-by or use-by dates; you smelt it or felt it! One day I climbed over the gate of the pigpen and threw some stale loaves over the top, then climbed back and hid them in a box until I finished my day's work. I then sneaked them out onto the field behind the bakery, retrieved them later and took them home to my starving family. I recall seeing the bearded pig farmer with his smelly open-top van and rotten crusts of bread falling from his trailer and insects were swarming all around the droppings, shaking his fist at me when he drove past...

But that bread delivery job came to abrupt end. About a mile from where we lived in Baguley was a posh estate known as the 'Spinney'. On one occasion, my boss left the van to make a delivery to one of the posh houses. I noticed a coin next to my seat and on closer inspection, it was a 'shilling'. I couldn't resist the temptation to remove it from the board and put it into my pocket. I thought to myself, one whole shilling will supply us with gas for a couple of hours. But I was in for a nasty shock, when the bread man returned, he took one look at the empty space where the coin had been, then turned to look to me, and without even saying a word, slapped me around the back of my head, and shouted at me to get out of the vehicle and piss off. I had to walk the long-distance home in the pouring rain, holes in my shoes, without any pay, and out of a job. I realised that it was a set-up, one of the customers must have recognised me from my own neighbourhood and told my boss not to trust me, and I fell for it.

The years passed...

Mam was still scrubbing the kitchen floor on her hands and knees as I pushed the door open and wheeled in an old bike I'd found on the field. I thought if I could build and repair this bike I could sell it for a few quid.

'Get out of here,' she screamed, 'I won't tell you again - get that bike out of here, off my kitchen floor.'

I held out my hands and waved back in defeat. 'Okay, okay, I will fix it round the back, it needs a few parts, I can use it for my paper round, mam.'

'I don't care, just get out of here. I've just mopped the floor you sod. Where's the money you got from last week's paper round and the bread round? I need it or we can't have any tea tonight. Come on, come on, I want it now; there's no food in the house; if you spent it on cigs I'll kill you, I'm warning you - where's that money?'

'I've only got ten bob,' I protested.

'What do you mean you've only got ten bob? You worked last week at every job, and how much did you get paid? Hand it over now!' She took all my money from me and said, 'Here's a shilling. Go and get lost.'

I stared at the coin and back at Mam. 'That doesn't leave me much, does it? How can I fix my bike with no money?'

'I don't give a damn about your stupid bike - there's no food in the house, and apart from your father, you're the only one that brings in any money at the moment. Go to the butchers and ask him for some scrag ends,' (old pieces of scrap meat). 'Here's a shilling, then go to the greengrocers and ask for some pot herbs - as much as you can, and spend the full shilling.

'If there's any change left, you can buy a penny mix and share it with your mates, if that's what you call 'em.'

'Okay, Mam, don't let nobody touch my bike.'

She flapped her hands at me impatiently, 'I won't, just get going or there will be no food for anybody.'

I'm sick of her picking on me all the time, what about the others in this house? It's always me, me, me ...

I was the 'unlucky' thirteen-year-old. My sisters and Michael were too young to be taking on any responsibilities and of the two elder brothers, Arthur was at sea and David was always out getting drunk with his girlfriend. I was the ideal candidate. On my way to get the errands done at the local shops, I went around the back of them before going for the food to see if I could find any old bike parts. I had to be careful as my mam would have been able to see me had I gone down the passage. As I passed the end of the shops, there was a puddle of water from the overnight rain and as I walked past it, I could see papers floating on the top. They looked like little toy rafts or boats bobbing on the puddle. As I got nearer, I could see what looked like a ten bob note. I was excited. I waded into the icy rainwater and could feel it seeping into my old shoes. That didn't bother me. I put my hand down into the grubby water and grabbed this piece of crumpled wet brown paper. Yes, it was a real ten bob note.

As I stuffed it into my pocket, I stopped and looked around to see if anybody had noticed me picking it up, but there was nobody there. Now I had all the money back that my mam had just taken from me. *There's no way she's going to know about this*. I could fix my bike and buy some sweets and a packet of fags and she would never know.

When I got back home, I gave her the food from the shops so that she could start cooking our tea, then I went upstairs, put my hand in my pocket and retrieved this crumpled wet note. I put it in the top of the airing cupboard so that it would dry out overnight.

This is the puddle where I found my ten bob note

The next morning, I woke up early, jumped up out of bed and made my way down the short hallway to the airing cupboard, but I had to be careful because some of the floorboards were loose and they creaked. (I think my brother Arthur might have hidden his loot from one of his naughty antics under there!) As I reached up and grabbed the note, it made a crackling noise like the breaking of a crisp; it had dried out all right! I folded it up and put into my pocket thinking how I would keep hold of it for a few days before I started to spend it like a kid in a toy shop, just so my mam wouldn't notice my sudden wealth.

Nowadays, my job as an ambulance driver provides me with the opportunity to revisit those areas where I used to play in the area around Wythenshawe Hospital. This draws on my memory and ignites it with flashbacks to those times when I used to be knee-deep in mud trying to drop the plants and keep up with the farmer during my Sunday market garden job. I can visualise the moments when his wife used to make tea and cakes for our short breaks and this was the only time that I had drank from cups that weren't dirty or cracked. Just for that moment, I felt special, but also very guilty that I was living the life of the well-off and not having to share it with my family.

I recall one of the farm workers asking me if I wanted to go and look at some cars with him after work. I jumped at the chance, but I knew that I didn't have any other jeans to wear, other than what I had on and they were filthy. I thought if I could leave work a bit early, I could cycle home, wash my dirty jeans and try and dry them in front of the fire. Off I went, but I couldn't get the dirt from the creases on the legs because they were too ingrained. When the man called round to pick me up, they were still soaking wet. I think he could see this, but he spared me the shame. Today, some fifty years on, I frequently pass the same area where I worked on those back-breaking chores. I can still smell the scents of the flowers that I used to dip into huge empty barrels filled with freezing cold water that had a dye mixed within it to change the colour from white to pink/red/orange and various other colours of flowers that I immersed into the vats because daisies only bloomed naturally in white. As for my one and only pair of jeans and T-shirt, they looked like the colours of the rainbow. I must have been the only kid wearing multi-coloured jeans, It wasn't fair. The world was a big scary playground but here I was trudging about doing chores – no wonder everyone was laughing while I seethed in fury and frustration.

My elder brother Arthur had a job on a chicken farm before he went to sea. One day he told me to meet him near the old iron railway bridge next to the farm where he was working, near Butcher Lane in Baguley. He stole some eggs and passed them to me from the railway embankment. He put the eggs into a brown paper bag, which I hooked over my handlebars. I climbed on the bike and started pedalling as fast as the bike could go so I could get home where my mam was waiting to take the eggs from me for our tea. The bag bounced around as I tried to dodge the cobbles; not one single egg survived the journey back. The yolks were dripping onto my front wheel. The faster I rode, the more the gooey slime was splattering from the spokes of my wheel and splashing into my face. My mam was furious; she chased me down the garden path and when she caught up with me, I felt an almighty slap on the back of my head and my precious bike was lying in the nettles of our unkempt front garden. Mam screamed at me to go upstairs to bed and barked, 'Don't you come back down till tomorrow morning!' I was so cold and hungry. I wanted to sneak downstairs for something to eat but the risk of getting caught wasn't worth it and there was no food in the house anyway. The only thing that was in our freezing cold kitchen was the empty fridge …

The Wag Man (The School Truant Officer) & Me

I've heard it said many times that schooldays are the best times of our lives, but not for me. I hated the place: the system, the teachers, and above all the discrimination. By this, I mean the well-off who were treated and respected above children like myself born into poverty.

School dinners weren't something that I looked forward to, not because of the lousy food, but the thing that always sticks in my memory is how we were segregated into two separate queues when lining up in the playground for dinner. We were told to form two lines: one for those who had paid for lunch and the other line which was for free dinners. This procedure was enforced by having colour-coded meal tickets: one paid and one not paid. This labelled us as 'the poor', not just by the other kids, but by the teachers as well. It was like having a number stamped on my wrist, just like those poor prisoners from the concentration camps in WW2.

Another embarrassing time for me is when we had to do PE (physical education). We were sent into the changing rooms and told to change into our gym clothes, which was a daunting and humiliating experience for me because my parents could not afford any kit or sports clothes for me to wear. I was told to go and ask the head teacher if there were any spare or unwanted clothes that had been left in the lost property locker. Whatever I found it never fitted me; it was either too big or too small, so this made me stand out even more in the crowd.

We had swimming lessons but my trunks were hand-me-downs and each time I tried to climb out of the pool's freezing water, my trunks would slip down with the weight of the water to reveal my white skinny arse. In trying to conceal my private parts, my trunks looked more like a sack filled with potatoes not my backside. All the kids would laugh at me while I was trying to pull my trunks back up, they teased me on the way back to school on the bus, 'Hey Whittie, haven't you got a little white arse!' The heckles continued all the way back to school.

When the ice cream man played his tune as his van stopped opposite our house, it taunted us because we couldn't afford such luxuries. (I still hear that same evocative tune on today's ice cream vans.) Kids would stand in front of our window laughing and licking their ice lollies and ice creams, just to tease us.

School photo day loomed. It was a hot summer's day. Summer for most kids was the time when they could play out. But for me, this wasn't a pleasurable time of the year. My dress code left something to be desired and lacked the seasonal look. We were told to come to school for these class photographs in our best clothes. Yet, for me, my clothes were for all-year-round occasions. I dreaded school photo days. We were asked to go out to the front of the school playing fields and line up in a group, with the tallest at the back. Then the rest of the other kids would follow suit in the front rows. I just wanted to run off and hide somewhere. My mam dressed me in the best clothes that she could muster, but these were just hand-me-downs off our neighbours. What made it even more embarrassing for me was that I had to don a thick heavy tweed jacket to keep my dignity.

As for my footwear, my shoes were full of holes in the soles. As we couldn't afford new or even second-hand shoes, my dad purchased a DIY shoe repair kit. This consisted of a vintage cast iron cobbler's anvil stand and some strips of rubber that he acquired from some old wellington boots that weren't fit for purpose anymore. He would position our shoes/boots around this shoe anvil and while attempting to re-sole my shoes, would smear rubber glue over the old worn-out sole, then attempt to cut round the rubber in the shape of the underside of my shoes. But his cutting appliances were not up to the task. He then left the glue on the footwear to dry overnight.

The next morning, he would remove my newly 'recast' shoes from the shoe anvil to inspect his handy work. I asked him whether he had fixed my shoes because I needed them next morning for the school photograph. He replied that they were ready to use, and they looked like new. I turned the shoes over to inspect them and was horrified to see that the newly laid rubber soles were out of shape with the older worn inner leather soles and heels. It was like trying to fit a square peg in a round hole, they were out of line. Because my dad had tried his best with the tools that he had, and I was too frightened of him to complain, I told my mam that I was not wearing them for school, or at any other time.

I was the only one in a jacket! Top right.

When the group photograph was distributed soon after, I just wanted to screw it up and chuck it over the school fence on my way home. However, I already knew that my mam would tell me to return it back to my teacher because we could not afford it. This is why today there are no school or family photographs of me and my brothers and sisters. The featured school photo was donated to me by a patient that I was transporting home after a hospital appointment. She remembered me from my school days and she is also in this picture.

On occasions, we would have visits from the health department's school nurse who would look for any health issues, such as bad teeth or illnesses, and dredge through pupils' hair to look for head lice or nits which was common practice in those days. As soap and toothpaste were in short supply in my household, I usually got picked out with some kind of health issues which just added to the discrimination and segregation from the other children and which provided more humiliation.

On one occasion, the nurse asked me about the bits of white stuff on my scalp and she wanted to know what it was. I told her my dad always washed our head with carbolic soap. She gasped, 'Well! Tell your dad to rinse your head next time, or I will be coming around to see him...!' Why me? Always 'Whittie'! Always the drudge, always the butt of people's mockery and their jokes about the 'Whittaker family'.

I remember being sent to stand outside the classroom for not having any games kit. Then a male teacher just happened to be passing where I stood shivering in the cold corridor. He went into the classroom to chat to my teacher, who must have told him why she had sent me outside. He then reappeared brandishing a huge leather strap. Without even asking me for my side of the story, he told me to stretch my right arm out in front of me, then with an almighty crack, he lashed out and landed the strap across my wrist and hand. I gave out an almighty cry, but before I could recover, he repeated this outrage again and again. It seemed like an eternity before he stopped. He then marched away, leaving me in tears. My hand and wrist were black and blue. Looking back in anger, I just think that he wanted to show his masculinity to a female colleague, but I had to pay the price for that.

Due to the fact that I was the family 'chosen one', it was always me who missed school. It even got to the stage where the Wag Man (school educational officer) would constantly be at our front door questioning my mother as to why I had not attended school. However, she always seemed to have a valid answer to give him: family sickness, no clothes for school. Looking back however, these were just lame duck excuses to keep me at home so that I could run errands for her, and go banging on neighbours' doors while their fathers were out at work, requesting to borrow money that never was never repaid. Eventually it reached the point that the Wag Man wouldn't tolerate it anymore. He reported my mother to the education authorities with his recommendation that my mam and I should attend a court hearing, enforcing a summons that I attend all future lessons, otherwise I could be sent to an approved school for young offenders.

I attended court and both my mam and I received a warning. If I missed school between then and leaving when I reached fifteen, I would be sent away. Not long after the court appearance, I was wagging school again with Dirty Barry when we heard the sound of an approaching old moped It was the school welfare officer chugging along on his bike, which sounded like a sewing machine on its last legs. We could see him getting nearer and nearer. He looked like Cyril 'Blakey' Blake from the 1970's sitcom *On the Buses* and even had 'Blakey's' stammer. Barry suggested that we jump over a neighbour's garden and hide from him which we promptly did. We could just hear an asthmatic 'pop-pop' as his two-stroke bike wobbled past and he never saw us. As regards to my ongoing school attendance, I just kind of showed my face now and then until I finally left. After working three jobs, nearly all my earnings had to be handed over to my mam to contribute to feeding us all. Still, I did manage to stash the odd earnings for my own use now and then.

My pals, Dirty Barry, Bill and Norman, and me decided to pool our hidden money to buy a broken-down scrambler motorbike from a mechanic father of one of our mates. His skills came in handy for helping us to fix the bike's ongoing problems. We were business men at the age of thirteen! We had to find ways of transporting this gigantic machine (an 'AJS') over to the local fields near Baguley Hospital so that we could ride it on private land and nobody, the police or anybody else, could punish us for riding a motorbike underage, with no insurance, no road tax, no MOT - not to mention the noise it made with only half an exhaust pipe.

It was great fun, but the bike came with many mechanical problems that we had difficulties trying to fix. We were constantly asking our friend's dad to come over to the fields and bring it back to life. It didn't have a kick-start pedal, it had broken off. The only way to start this monster was to bump start it, and to do this, one of us lads would sit on the bike, while the others pushed it from behind while we inhaled the choking exhaust fumes. It didn't have the luxury of any brakes, lights, horn or any other basic functions of a roadworthy motorbike. But boy, did we draw the crowds! Kids would offer us sweets just to have a ride on the back. The sense of proprietorship sowed the seeds of an entrepreneurial spirit and looking back now, maybe this wealth could have motivated me into owning my own franchise business later in life. We had a great time being the talk of the neighbourhood. More important than all that, however, was that it created some pride and dignity that helped me overcome the slagging and abuse for having no decent clothes or games kit.

Life is different for me today. I can now appreciate how difficult it must have been for my parents to not only feed and clothe us all but to endure all the torments and discriminatory taunts from the neighbourhood and from outsiders. Nonetheless, at the age of around thirteen, I was too young to even care less about their situation. Maybe if they hadn't had so many of us, life could have been a lot better for me.

We were certainly no saints. Not far from where my mate Norman lived there was a footbridge leading from the Baguley district and over to Royal Oak. Just for laughs, me and my mates would hide under the walkway. We would wait until a woman would walk over the bridge then we would poke sticks through the gaps in the cross beams that were visible from underneath. We would eagerly wait for the screams from the unsuspecting victim.

There was one occasion when Norm spotted a bloke running from the nearby housing estate. He was bellowing, 'I will fucking kill you little perverted bastards when I get hold of you!' He was wielding what looked like a walking stick. As he got nearer his shouts became louder and more frightening. We legged it over the railway lines - the same tracks where we would collect coal that had fallen off the trains. We never ventured to that bridge again in fear of that mad man catching us.

Even today, I still don't understand why so many traumatic events happened to me when I was such a young age. Yet, there's one thing that still sticks in my mind: the time I was sent to a convalescent home in Lytham St Annes.

This is the bridge that divided Baguley from Royal Oak

This is the view from underneath the bridge with the cracks where we poked sticks through when the ladies walked over

The local health authority and education departments used to send children like myself away from home and family for two weeks to this institution. It was supposed to be a way of having a 'respite' holiday but it was nothing but a dumping ground for the mentally ill, the poor and the homeless. I still have flashbacks of the time I spent there. I had great difficulty sleeping properly. I missed the sounds and antics of my brothers and sisters. Even though we always fought and bickered when we were four in a bed, we had a great affection for each other, as we were literally all in it together. I missed them so much. I even thought that I might not ever see them again and this made me weep myself to sleep. I slept in a dormitory with children whose backgrounds were similar to my own. The memories I have are of this dark, dingy Tudor-style structure with the nursing staff dressed in uniforms like Florence Nightingale.

The home, situated on the sandbanks off the sea at Lytham St Annes, was not too far away from Blackpool Airport. I still can remember hearing the light aircraft taking off and landing. One memorable occasion was when we were taken to the amusement park at Blackpool. I had never seen fairground rides before and I looked at the soaring rides with dread and terror. The dodgems, the big wheel, and any other spinning or rotating structures turned my stomach round like the fast spin speed of a washing machine. I staggered off the big wheel and was violently sick - and that was meant to be a place where I was supposed to have a 'holiday'! I think it was more like a punishment as nobody looked after me. When I told them that I was upset and I wanted to go home to my mam, I was told to stop complaining and be grateful for where I had been sent. It wasn't much different to being sent to an approved school.

Bedtime couldn't come quick enough for me. It meant that when I woke up the next morning I was a day closer to going home. The dormitories were long, grim, forbidding and menacing. They had huge radiators along the dark, painted brick interior walls and the small single beds were spaced out like those of an army barracks. At night, I would stare up at the high Victorian, decorated ceilings with dangling, long flexes and naked lightbulbs that would have suited the Blackpool illuminations just down the road. Breakfast was a dish of thick porridge with a consistency of glutinous cement. Then there was the glass of milk to try to break up the lumps of porridge that couldn't find their way down into my swollen stomach. Often at some point in the night there would be shouts and cries from the mentally ill kids and this went on night after night. I remember one night in particular. I nearly jumped out of my skin, when I felt this hand on my face and somebody trying to climb onto my bed. I screamed for my mam and pushed who, or what was trying to scare me out of the way. I could feel the blanket being tugged away from me, as I tried to hold onto it, then suddenly all the lights came on and the nurses ran over and grabbed this screaming, handicapped kid and marched him out of the dorm.

After that night, I was very scared and frightened, not knowing if he would return after they removed him from the dorm. He was shouting and screaming as he was taken away. I woke that night screaming and crying out, 'Please don't, please, please don't take me, I will be good from now on!' but there weren't any staff around, so I just cried myself back to sleep. I never knew where they took him, but he never appeared in our dormitory again. The idea of this place was to give my mother a break and one less mouth to feed. It did the opposite for me. But when I returned home my mother just hugged me and said: 'I will never let you go there again!'

Blackburn convalescent home

Aunt Jessie

My dad never mentioned his half-sister (Aunt Jessie), but my mother did. She was our secret supplier of food and clothing. Not even her husband knew because I think she was scared in case he stopped her from seeing and feeding us. Even today, I'm not sure why he didn't know about us and I will never know, but one thing was for sure - she was our lifeline, providing much-needed supplies. There were no food banks in those days. South Manchester in the 1950s was no bed of roses.

Aunt Jessie was a lifesaver and we never forgot what she did for us. She was one of those people who only thought about others and not herself. Every Saturday morning, I was 'lumbered' (as I regarded it then) with meeting her in Manchester city centre. My regular bus trip was on the 101 from where I lived in Baguley which took around half an hour. Whenever it was raining, my mother would make me don a plastic see-through folded headscarf. I had no say in the matter; my mam would peer through the damp-stained net curtains, and watch me board the bus from the living room (through the only remaining window that wasn't cracked), to make sure that I didn't take it off. Our window frames were made of metal, so in the summer they would expand, and in the winter, they would contract, so if we had a period in between, it was just about possible to open them. This was a very embarrassing moment for me, especially when my friends used to hang out in the bus shelter, smoking the remains of a fag or 'dimp' that they had scavenged from the pavements. It was known as kerb-stone blend.

After boarding the double-decker bus, with its grab-rail in the centre of the aisle, the bus conductor asked me where I was going and my destination. 'Town,' I replied.

'That'll be one and thruppence,' (six-and-a-half pence), which was half of what my mother had given me for my bus fare.

As the bus pulled into the Piccadilly station, I could see my Aunt Jessie, making her way over to greet me on my arrival. She was about 5ft 6in tall, with dark mousy hair. She constantly had a smile on her face, and had a slight hump in her back, yet was always in a hurry to go nowhere fast. She would board the bus, even before it had come to a stop. I used to pretend that she wasn't looking for me, not that I was ashamed to have an aunt like her, but when she scurried her way down the aisle and slapped a big, wet, sloppy kiss on my forehead, I screwed up my face and wanted to be anywhere else but on that bus. When we alighted, she took my hand and hurried me across Piccadilly Gardens and into Paulden's (the department store where Debenham's is currently sited in Market Street) where we had to push our way through the weekend shoppers, often women dressed in their finery or 'fur coats and no knickers' as my mam used to say.

'Who do they think they are? They're no different from us,' Aunt Jessie would fume.

'And as for their pathetic little hen-pecked husbands they're a poor excuse for a man.'

Poor old Aunt Jessie, she was looking tired after a short trip on the 192 bus from Piccadilly to Levenshulme. We would walk through the crowcroft park to her house, which was a modest semi-detached house with toffee-shop bay windows.

It had panoramic views across the road overlooking a creepy old church, which scared the life out of me when it rang out its eerie bells. I never met her husband, Uncle Robert, but I was led to believe that he was a high-ranking police officer, and about six foot two, with a muscular physique, and a very deep voice.

'Quick, Uncle Robert's here, you can't be seen in this house, he doesn't know about you and your family,' she cried.

Jessie would push me into the pantry. I was petrified, cowering fearfully in the pitch-dark dungeon. I could hear the big grandfather clock chiming. After what seemed like a lifetime hiding in this dark, claustrophobic cupboard, the only way I could see what was going on was to peer through the crack in the old wooden door.

'Alan are you okay?' she asked.

I was terrified at the thought of this giant of a man catching me in the cupboard. I wet myself and it was running down my legs, I was so scared. What if he took me away to his police station for stealing his food and locked me up in a cell? I wouldn't ever see my mam and dad and family again! I thought I saw a huge silhouette of a man standing next to my Aunt Jessie. He was enormous. My knees were knocking. I was so afraid that he might hear my sounds and snatch open the pantry door.

I was trying to cower as low as I could in case Uncle Robert opened the door. I must have knocked something on the shelves because I could feel something dripping onto my head: sticky just like jam or something. I could smell the fruit of its contents and could whiff the freshly baked cakes. This made me hungry but I didn't dare reach for them. There was silence then she said, 'It's okay, he's not here yet.'

The looming figure must have been a figment of my imagination.

'Would you like some cake and a glass of milk?' she would call out.

'Yes, please Aunt Jessie,' I replied eagerly.

As usual, Jessie was full of concern for my family,

'How are things at home? Do you have enough clothes for school?'

'We just have to make do with hand-me-downs,' I replied.

'What about your mam and brothers and sisters? How are they doing?'

I was only a child, burdened with responsibility at too young an age. The floodgates opened.

'Ok, the house gets very cold in the winter, and there's no money for the gas and electric meters, but I know that I shouldn't be telling you this. David has a way of opening the meters, and removing some shillings to be reused on other days, when there's no money.' (That was usually every day.)

'Arthur's been in trouble again with the police, he was caught stealing food from the local grocers, the police have been round to the house again; my mam protects him, and tries to keep my dad from finding out.'

I could see tears glistening in her eyes from the ceiling light, and she told me: 'One day things will get better for all of you and you will grow up to be a kind and generous man.' I like to think her wishes have come to pass.

Aunt Jessie made sure I would never meet Uncle Robert and even today when I pass the bus stop where we used to get off the 192 and walk the short distance to her house, I wonder why she never allowed me or my family to meet Uncle Robert. Was he really that bad? Or was it just dear old Aunt Jessie keeping him to herself? Maybe she was embarrassed because she and Uncle Robert had a nicer house than us, and she didn't want to make us feel humiliated. It could simply be that she didn't want her husband to ever find out about the other, darker side of her life.

Amidst these hard times, happy times, frightening times, there was a child being moulded, learning to cope with the taunts and often nasty banter, being hardened so to speak, but never realizing it at the time – just hurting. The kids doing the bullying would be victims themselves if they didn't assert themselves. I had already experienced a lot of knocks and more were to follow. But my life was to expand way beyond the confines of Wythenshawe to places I could only have imagined.

I never really knew my dad. What I can always remember about him is that he was a tall man, well-built and he wouldn't take any nonsense from anybody. He always put his family first no matter what the difficulties must have been like for him and my mam.

This picture is the only [undated] photograph of my father that I know of

I remember looking back with happiness at the times he used to take me into Manchester. He would go into Yates' pub just around the corner from the old Woolworths' building and tell me to stand at the door while he went in to have a pint of beer. This was about his only luxury apart from the fags, but he wasn't a selfish man. I recall that he used to check on me to see if I was okay. Standing outside, he would bring me a bottle of lemonade and a pork pie. This was the treat that I looked forward to and I keep that memory of him today when I eat a pork pie.

After my dad passed away, my mam was taken to hospital because she had serious kidney problems. However, it was also discovered that she was pregnant again. At the age of around thirteen I didn't really understand how or why she would want another child. But the doctors at the time decided that because there was no father at home, the baby would have been too much for my mother to deal with along with her sickness. The decision was made by all involved along with my two elder brothers David and Arthur that the child would have to be put up for adoption.

Today, I realise that this must have been heart-breaking for my mam, but in hindsight, I don't think she would have had any say in the matter. My elder brothers David and Arthur would have also been devastated. Even they wouldn't have been able to convince or persuade the doctors to allow my mam and the family to keep this child. I believed at the time that the young baby was a girl and my brother Arthur gave her the name of 'Christine'. How my mam coped with all this, on top of worrying about her children at home without her, I do not know. Strange as it might seem I never really wanted to visit my mam while she was sick in hospital. When I finally did visit her, I recall her asking me why I hadn't visited before now. I didn't really have an answer. Maybe I was blaming her for bringing another child into our family, and another mouth to feed, because there was barely enough food and clothing to feed the rest of us. Later on, however, I began to feel guilty and ashamed for not going to see my mam when she needed me most.

We never knew what happened to our lovely sister Christine, and we never heard from her. As I grew older I began to stop thinking about her. I'm not sure why this was; maybe it was just over time, and I never saw her anyway so I couldn't have a picture of her in my mind.

CHAPTER TWO

ADOLESCENCE: 'PEANUT FACTORY' NATIONAL SEA TRAINING COLLEGE

It was a Friday morning and I received a letter, I shouted to my mam that I had got it and I was going away to the training college. There was no answer.

'I'm going,' I said firmly.

'You're going where?'

'To the college.'

'What are you talking about?'

'Here is the letter, look, the letter and my train ticket. I've been keeping it from you because I know that if you had seen it, you would probably have hidden it from me, or even worse still, torn it up. I travel there on Sunday.'

She cried, 'You can't. You're not old enough.'

'Yes, I am, I'm sixteen now, that's the age requirement to join the Merchant Navy.'

'Who has put you up to this?'

'Nobody has.'

'You liar, it's your brother, Arthur.'

'No, Mam, it's not Arthur, it's about me. It could be the beginning of my new life away from all this poverty and having to be your errand boy and the breadwinner for all my brothers and sisters; a chance to see the world and get paid for it. I think what you're really not happy about is that there won't be anybody here to replace me, and to be at your beck and call all the time. That's what this is all about. Well, I'm going, and not you or anybody else will hold me back. Oh, and don't try and make me feel guilty, Mam, because I'm not falling for it.'

Sunday morning arrived; suitcase packed and I was off - this was it. I looked back, and as I turned the door handle, I saw the disappointed look on my mam's tearful, sad face. As I approached the front gate, I turned around for one last time, I could see the old net curtains move, I knew she was there watching me, probably hoping that I wouldn't go.

But despite her anger, I knew that she would get used to the idea of me going to sea, especially when I returned home after long trips away, handing her some of my wages, and gifts from abroad. She was very good at manipulating me. Despite her looking upset, I felt the need to say to her: 'It's my turn now, Mam. I'm off.'

Looking back now it must have taken a lot of courage to speak to my mam as I did then. I always wanted to tell my mother about the way in which everything seemed to be landed on my shoulders, but I was afraid of hurting her. As I grew older, I realised how difficult life was for her and that she needed as much help and support as she could get, and that's where my jobs came in as an additional income.

Attached to the letter was a ticket to London and another one to travel to Gravesend, Kent, along with directions, instructions on how to get there, information about whom I would meet on arrival at Gravesend, and where I would take a bus along with all the 'new peanuts' to the training college. All newbies at the sea school were called 'Peanuts' because we were classed as being wet behind the ears. Nonetheless, this was an exciting time for me, but also a frightening event as I had never really left home before.

My Seaman's Discharge Book

Upon arrival at Manchester Piccadilly station, I hadn't a clue where to go and what to do. Everything looked huge: the many platforms, and waiting trains with their massive locomotives puffing out big grey clouds of smoke and the peak-capped ticket man who beckoned me to walk towards him. He glanced at my ticket and pointed to the train standing on platform three.

'Go on laddie,' he shouted, 'run or you'll miss the train, no more till tomorrow.'

I ran as quickly as I could, towing my heavy suitcase. As I climbed aboard a luxurious coach, the guard looked at my ticket and said, 'You're in first class boy, you need to go to the back and sit in third class.'

I grabbed the case and shuffled my way down the aisle until I reached the far end of the train where there were other passengers seated on the grubby, worn-torn seats. As I looked out of the steamy windows, I wiped the glass in the middle into a small, square shape. I could see the conductor waving a flag, he blew on his whistle and the train started to move, shunting slowly at first, then it began to gather pace, billowing clouds of grey smoke casting a shadow over my carriage as it moved slowly forward. I felt excited but a little frightened about what the day and the next three months would have in store for me. I hadn't really eaten any breakfast, but my mother had given me some 'butties' and a bottle of pop to keep me going until I reached Gravesend. Still, what she didn't know is that I had saved some of my pocket money and hidden it from her. I had about £5 and a sixpence and thrupenny bit (the latter being three-and-a-half pence respectively). When I opened the brown paper bag that had my lunch inside, a piece of paper fell onto my lap. It was my mam's handwriting.

Dear Alan, I hope that you have a safe journey and you get to your college without getting lost, I know I was a bit angry with you when you told me you were going away to sea but I love you so much and I will miss you. Please write to me when you arrive there, love Mam.

It was about six o'clock that evening when I finally arrived at the school. My first day at the sea college is one that I will never forget. The other spotty, pale-faced 'peanuts' and I disembarked from the old bus, which looked like it had just been rescued from the scrapyard. We marched single file to the main gates of the dingy building with the aura of a penitentiary. As we approached the entrance we were taunted and insulted by the trainees who were hanging out of the windows and calling out,

'Hey Peanuts, hey Peanuts, you aren't ever going home!' As I looked back, I could see the old bus pulling away and driving off into the distance. Now I knew that there was no going back. This was it. Was my mam right? Should I have stayed home with her?

I picked up my suitcase and headed towards the entrance. *Three months*, I kept saying to myself. *That's all it is - ninety days, am I going to get through this?*

But I was determined. As I walked in through the main entrance, I peeped through two large double doors. I was summoned inside by a very tall and stern looking man in uniform and I went through the formality of giving my name so that I could be struck off the list.

'Welcome to the National Sea Training School.' He spoke with a southern accent and very formal manner. 'All deck trainees will complete a twelve-week intensive course on seamanship which is put together in modules.'

I didn't say anything but I did not know what 'modules' meant. I never inquired because I didn't want to look stupid on my first day.

'This includes lifeboat training which will take place on the river Thames. As this is January you will feel the full force of our Kent winter, ha,ha!' (I think he enjoyed saying that.)

'But for the rest of the evening you can all make your way to the mess room and sample the grub that your fellow peanut stewards have been cooking for all us unfortunate guinea pigs. If you survive this, you will make it to the twelfth week of this course!'

Then it was time to turn in for my first night's sleep. I will never forget that first night in the dorm. Just as I was about to drop off after a very long day, all hell broke loose. The lights were switched on. I was in the top bunk and there was a lad below on the bottom bed. There were shouts and screams coming from all directions and the next thing I knew, I felt the full force of somebody battering me over the head with a pillow. After what seemed a lifetime, all went quiet, but I could see the debris of a pillow, which had burst and disintegrated all over my bunk.

We were informed by the officers that if anybody was caught fighting or misbehaving throughout our time there, we would be sent home. There were boxing grudge-fight nights. This was the procedure to stop boys fighting in the school so it would also be staged as entertainment for all to see. Most of the time, it was a mismatch that would end up in tears for the loser. Of course, I fell into that category!

Weekends meant shore leave with trips into the local town, Denton, where we stood out from the locals with our cropped hair and uniforms. There was always trouble with the local boys: fights and name-calling because we stole their girlfriends.

When we returned back to the school, we were put on detention and forfeited our next leave. We were also "sentenced to Jenkers' (scrubbing duties.) Eventually things became too much for me. I am not sure if I was just homesick, or feeling guilty about not being at home to help my mam with the upkeep of our family; everything seemed to land on my shoulders and weighed me down. I went along to see the Chaplain who was the one person in whom I could confide and trust. I opened up to him with my anxieties and my emotions. He persuaded me not to give up and to carry on with the rest of the course. He said that if I gave in now, I would regret it when I returned home, and probably for the rest of my life. It would be even worse seeing my big brother Arthur return home after his voyages from afar. When I think back on that conversation with the Chaplain, I'm glad that I never quit. The encounter had a profound impact on the positive way in which I think now: never to quit when the going gets tough. What a great favour that man did for me then and now...

*I was given permission from the lad on the right to use this picture.
Me on the left – 1968*

CHAPTER THREE

MY FIRST SHIP – M V MANCHESTER PORT

I had left the gates of the 'Peanut factory' and entered the gates of 'Manchester Docks' back in the north where my new life was about to begin. As I walked down Trafford Road carrying two substantial brown battered suitcases containing all my worldly goods, I felt nervous but also excited about my new life in the Merchant Navy. I had to call into the shipping federation building just off Trafford Road to undergo a medical check. This was only a matter of dropping my trousers in front of the doctor, who then said, 'cough'. Being naïve, I didn't know I was being told to cough. I thought that he might be checking to see whether I had a cold or not; why would you want me to drop my trousers and check down below, I thought? However, I did as I was told. I was then informed that I had to call at the union office a little bit further down the road. After I got the 'all-clear' from the union, I continued my walk towards the solid white structure of the dock gate (the structure is still there today). Upon entering, I was stopped by the security police. After getting the all-clear, he pointed the way down to number nine dock, which was the largest of all the wharfs in Salford.

There were many ships lined up along the never-ending dock; most of them were 'Manchester Liners'. After passing several vessels that were berthed, I spotted this massive black hull with the name *Manchester Port* on her bow in white lettering. WOW!!! Was I really going to be sailing on this monster? As I approached the gangway, it swayed from side to side in the strong winds blowing across the docks. I boarded the steps whilst carrying my cases up to the top. The gangway guide ropes were slack so I had great difficulty trying to reach the top whilst freighted down by my meagre luggage.

Once on board I just didn't know which way to go to find my cabin so I carried on up the stairway, which led me into the officer's bar. I knew this because they were all wearing white shirts with gold braid on their jacket sleeves (just like the officers at the sea school). I thought that I could join them for a drink but I was in for a shock. One of them stood up and made it quite clear that the crew did not have a bar. So, I was in for a nasty shock. I was confronted by this stuck-up, snotty-nosed pillock, dressed in white shorts and shirt (with no ranking distinctions of any sort). He weighed me up-and-down with a smirk on his polka-dot face. As I asked where my cabin was located, it was evident to him that I was 'uneducated', so he put me in my place and suggested that I 'go below' (about four decks) and join the crew to sign-on. This was a short and unceremonious procedure, it was just a matter of signing my name, even though this wasn't easy for me with my poor writing skills. This was just to confirm that I was signing up to their ship's articles (terms and conditions). It all seemed a bit farcical.

I eventually found my cabin which was about the size of a small broom cupboard with a porthole which looked as though it leaked, with rust stains around its circular rim. The cabin was located at the stern of the ship next to the propeller shaft that ran between our cabin and a smelly old rope locker. There were two bunks, with about two feet distance from each other and two little cupboards that were meant to accommodate all my worldly goods. Pipes ran from one end of the deck-head (ceiling) to the other; it was evident that they had not been cleaned since the ship was first launched. Cobwebs clustered with dead insects hung from the pipes. As my cabin mate was yet to appear, I chose the bottom bunk; no doubt this would be an issue once I did meet my fellow deck boy. One thing I learnt from the sea school was how to make my bunk. The bedding was lying folded on top of my stained thin mattress: two old torn sheets, one stained pillow case and one brown blanket with moth holes and torn edges. These must have been left from the previous peanuts. I wasn't sure if this was an improvement from my earlier years at home.

It was then time to explore the accommodation - which was daunting. The lighting was very dim and eerie. Every time I walked through a doorway, which was dark and dingy, I had to feel my way along the bulkheads to find my way along to each doorway entrance. There were so many watertight doors and portholes that I became dizzy and confused. Nevertheless, I could tell by the grubby interior of the alleyways that this was all the crew's quarters.

After spending my first night's sleep onboard a ship, the next morning all the rest of the crew arrived on board. All the ABs (able seamen) looked like they had just been dragged up from 'Davie Jones's locker' (a term used by seamen as something dredged up from the seabed). Eventually, I found the crew's mess room and once inside I looked around and could see what looked like a serving hatch, which led through to the galley. There were several tables and chairs which had chains underneath the seats and fastening hooks. I figured out that these hooks were to secure the chairs for when we hit bad weather (not looking forward to that). The tables had folding sides along the edges which clipped together to stop our plates and cutlery from sliding off. Eventually, the messroom started to fill with sailors of all nationalities. They weren't a beautiful sight: unshaven, long greasy hair and dirty jeans splattered with all colours of paint. The closer they got to me, the more I could smell the stench of stale booze and fags. Now it was time for me to start asking questions, but I was nervous and too frightened to speak to anybody. This wasn't a very good start. Still, I had to have some dialogue with my future crewmates.

My first conversation was with the mess man whose job it was to look after the crew and help the sailors and others. I asked him what time we would be eating our lunch and he replied, 'with about seven bells'. (The ship's bells are a system to indicate the time.)

How the hell am I supposed to know what that means, I thought?

'Have you signed on yet?' he enquired.

'Not yet,' I replied.

He raised an eyebrow. 'You need to go to the 'Old Man's' cabin and sign on, just follow the stairway further up from the officer's bar, then one deck higher, make sure you knock first, you don't want to piss the Old Man off before you sign on.'

At the top of the stairway there was a sturdy mahogany door with a brass name plate above announcing, 'The Captain'. I hesitated before I could muster up the courage to knock, then I did so only very hesitantly.

'Yes, who's that?' a husky voice boomed.

'Alan Whittaker, Sir, I've come to sign on.'

'What's your rating boy?'

'Deck boy, Sir, first trip.'

'Well don't just stand there boy, muttering! In you come.'

I entered his cabin, it looked like something that I had seen in films about luxury cruise liners with their stately suites for the super-rich.

'Sign here, boy,' he muttered. He kept his head down, so I didn't see much of his face.

'Will you be making an allotment?'

An allotment? That's what I was working on back in the garden centre, I thought. 'Not sure, Sir.' I think that he wanted to save me the embarrassment of not knowing what he meant.

'Will you be sending any of your pay home to your mother?'

'Oh, yes, Sir, I've got to.'

'Then how much will you be sending her?'

'I think about four pounds and ten shillings a month.'

'Ok, just sign here and the money will go out to your mother every calendar month.'

'Calendar month, what's that, Sir? Never heard that expression before!'

'It means every full month on the calendar!'

'Yes, Captain, that will be okay.'

After that ordeal I returned to the messroom, then out of nowhere this huge man appeared in the doorway. I wasn't good with accents, but having just left sea school I mixed with all sorts: Geordies, Scousers, Scots, Irish, and Welsh. I figured out that this man was a Welshman. He was enormous, his husky gravel voice was enough to scare the hell out of any new peanuts like me. He turned out to be the ship's bosun. He called out to everybody in the room to 'standby fore and aft', as the ship was about to leave and beckoned me to follow him up to the front of the vessel, that is the fo'c'sle head. This was my station for the rest of the voyage and was where all the mooring ropes and ship's anchors were located. The bosun told me to help the sailors with releasing the mooring ropes, which meant taking the ropes off the 'bits' (the post that the ropes were wrapped around). I just followed the lads around like a lost sheep.

Then, all of a sudden, I heard this deafening sound coming from the bridge, followed by filthy grey smoke billowing out of the huge funnel. This was it, we were off - my first time at sea. I could smell the fumes that were blowing towards us as I looked over the side. I could see the filthy waters churning around the bow with the tugboat dredging up the filth when it opened up its noisy engines.

The mate's radio crackled, the call came from the bridge, 'Single up to headline and a spring' (a term used to describe the wire rope that held the ship alongside as leverage to move the vessel forward or aft). I didn't have a clue what the orders meant so I just followed the rest. Then the order came to 'let go all ropes'. Next thing I heard was the bosun screaming at me.

'Get out of those fucking bights you fucking idiot!' (The bights were the loops of the wire coiled up on the deck.) If one of the loops had tightened up around my ankles, I would have been in a lot of pain). As I jumped out of the way of the incoming wire rope, one of the able seamen (AB) told me never to stand in the bight of a running rope.

The tug wire that was pulling us round to face the other way was creaking as it became taut. I could see into the little wheelhouse of the boat where the man on the wheel had a long black beard. I just made out a scar-across his forehead before he looked up at me and growled. I ducked behind the big steel breakwater so he couldn't see me, then the massive ship started to swing around ready to move forward to the first lock. As the ship approached the lock, our tug released its wire rope so that it could enter the smaller lock which lay parallel to the one we maneuvered into. We tried to coil the heavy mooring ropes that were coming through the fairleads (rollers) but they were soaking wet after the linesman had let them go into the filthy waters. My working clothes left much to be desired and were now almost beyond repair but I had no spares.

It was fascinating to watch the water in the lock chamber as our ship began to descend, allowing us to leave the first lock, which was Mode Wheel, once the level had dropped enough to open the gates. Once opened, we could slowly move out from the lock. Simultaneously, our tugs were waiting for us to lower the wire rope so that it could be attached. The powerful little boats towed the ship away from the dock to escort us towards the second lock, Barton, whilst our vessel sailed slowly down the Manchester Ship Canal. There were many sightseers along the banks of the ship canal with some waving at us as we sailed past. The bosun told me that the ship had to be steered along the centre of the canal so as not to run aground. That short conversation was about the only time that I recall ever being spoken to in a friendly manner by a petty officer.

This was a moment that I would always remember fondly. I could hear the engines firing up and black clouds of smoke rising from the funnel. The smell of the fumes was something that I had never experienced before, and won't ever forget. The thick clouds of soot sticking to the mast and derricks were like confetti when thrown in the air, only to land on whoever happened to be in the vicinity of its fallout. As I looked over the side, all-the flotsam and jetsam resting on the surface was being churned up only to settle again as we passed on our stately progress down the Ship Canal.

I was kind of excited, but felt a little useless and confused about what was going on around me. Scary, and yet so different from what I had learned at the sea school. As the ship made its way slowly towards Irlam Locks there was a lot of activity and commotion going on around me and I kept on tripping over the uncoiled ropes that were lying scattered all over the deck.

A quote from BBC England *Seven Wonders*:

'The Manchester Ship Canal is a great example of how engineering helped the North West to become an industrial powerhouse. Construction started in November 1887 and took seven years to complete, with Queen Victoria opening the canal in 1894. The canal runs for 36 miles from Eastham on the Mersey estuary to Salford in Greater Manchester. The Manchester Ship Canal is best described as a 'linear port', providing access for shipping to docks along its length. The canal is also known as the 'Big Ditch', because of the immense size of the building project. It was dug virtually by hand by teams of 'navvies' - workers on the navigation or the canal.

Many workers died in the brutal working conditions. The canal uses much of the route of the Mersey and Irwell Navigation. The Barton Swing Aqueduct was constructed to replace Brindley's earlier, pioneering stone aqueduct across the Irwell. As well as the aqueduct, the Ship Canal has seven swing road bridges, five high level railway viaducts, and four high level road bridges. It also boasts five sets of huge locks - Eastham, Latchford, Irlam, Barton and Mode Wheel.

The engineering brilliance of the canal enabled ocean-going vessels to navigate their way from the Irish Sea into the industrial heart of Manchester. The canal is still a working waterway, although the number of ships making their way from the mouth of the Mersey to Salford Quays has declined.'

As the ship approached the opening of the next lock, Latchford, we slipped the wires of the tugboats off the bits, so we could manoeuvre into the very tight, confined space of the first lock. And there was only one more lock, Eastham, before we reached the end of the canal. At the same time, the tugboats entered into a smaller lock parallel to the one we were in. We passed two ropes down to the lot gatekeepers who moored our ship into the lock. Slowly the ship began to descend further into the lock basin and I could see water leaving the lock space so the ship would be at the same level as the canal on the other side of the lock gates. When this procedure was completed, the forward gate opened and we once again tied up to the tugs, then continued our passage until we reached the River Mersey, which was our gateway to the Irish Sea and then onto the North Atlantic.

After leaving the ship canal, the magnificent and historic city of Liverpool appeared on the starboard side of the ship. This was the first time, apart from going to Gravesend in Kent, that I had seen somewhere different from my home.

Looking over and beyond Liverpool, I could see a lot of old buildings: docks with wooden sheds stacked with timber, and other freight that must have come from overseas.

At last my life seemed to be taking a better course - literally. I could feel the ship moving along and lurching from side to side whilst leaving Liverpool which was disappearing in our wake. The motion of the ship started to increase and at this point I'm not sure if I was already beginning to feel seasick, or whether it was just my imagination and the worst was still to come.

I didn't sleep very well that first night aboard ship with all the rolling and pitching motion of the vessel. I could hear loose objects rolling from side to side in our cabin. As I leaned over my bunk sleepy-eyed, I could see my cabin mate violently throwing up. This had an immediate effect on me and now my stomach started to turn. The smell and stench of his vomit, along with the stink from the rope locker, smelt more like the contents of the garbage bin from the galley. I could see the slime dripping from my cabin mate's mouth and his eyes were like piss holes in the snow. I wanted to use the sink myself, because it was a long walk down the alleyway to the bathroom. However, the thought of using the sink just after my mate had thrown up all over the place rapidly changed my mind. I wanted to clear the cobwebs from my eyes and brush my teeth but as I approached the sink, the smell was unbearable. The contents of his stomach lined the sink bowl and looked like a mixture of rotten vegetables, porridge, and whatever else had appeared from the bilges of his stomach. I decided not to use the sink; it would have just made me feel worse than I already felt. Just as I hauled myself back up to my bunk, there was an almighty bang on our door. I just froze as I didn't have a clue what the time was.

'Hey, you pair of cock suckers, wakey-wakey, get your sorry arses out of your pit, and go to the mess room. There's some greasy eggs and bacon in the oven; it will settle your guts, ha-ha,' jeered the bosun.

I opened my shoebox-like cupboard to get my working clothes which were piled up in a heap. I scrambled into them and made my way to the door, brushing past my pale-faced cabin mate. He looked like he had been dredged from the bottom of the ocean, not a pretty sight. I made my way along the dark alleyway, but the ship was rolling so badly that I felt I was walking up the bulkheads, not the deck. As I entered the messroom, I looked around at all the bearded and unshaven, shabby looking seamen. I was still in early puberty so I hadn't got to the stage where I shaved; it was obvious that they were going to make fun of me.

I managed to eat a piece of toast to line my empty stomach. The bosun told me to go with two of the able seamen to start battening down the deck cargo. (securing the cargo). We staggered along the starboard side of the foredeck, the waves lashing over the rails and onto the deck. Just as I tried to climb over some ropes and wires, a huge wave towered over the side of the ship, but the seamen knew how to dodge it, and of course, I didn't. I got absolutely soaked and I could hear laughter from the men ahead of me. From then on, I knew that it was going to be like this until I finished my first trip.

As the days went by I still felt very seasick, and so did my cabin mate. The only thing I looked forward to was climbing into my bunk after my day's work, without really having had anything much to eat. There was a deadlight which blocked out any light from the porthole. But this had to be clamped down very tight so as not to let any other light enter our cabin. The strange thing about our cabin was that it was located at the lower end of the stern of the ship, so the swell would wash up against the glass on the porthole. The sea would lash up against the ship's side, which made our cabin very dark until the waves dropped. This was quite strange because the rays of light from the moon would illuminate the cabin for a split second, spreading beams of light across the bulkheads. I was told that the North Atlantic could be very cruel, especially in the winter, but I hadn't expected anything like this. I had watched films when I was in the sea school, about ships sailing across the seas. I think they must have deliberately kept quiet about the ferocious seas of the North Atlantic. On many dark nights, I would stare through the porthole just to see if there were any more ships on the horizon. Sometimes my mind would play tricks on me. I would often drift back into the times when I was at home and my mam would bawl at me for bringing my treasured bike into the kitchen, but these thoughts soon disappeared. Maybe I was just subconsciously trying to block her out of my new life.

After we had been at sea for about six days the weather seemed to improve slightly. Eventually the ship settled down and stayed on a steady course. Most of my working days were spent helping the ABs, and assisting them with their daily task of washing down the decks, the cranes and the derricks. I think I would have endured a better treatment in a labour camp than I did from these hairy-arsed sailors.

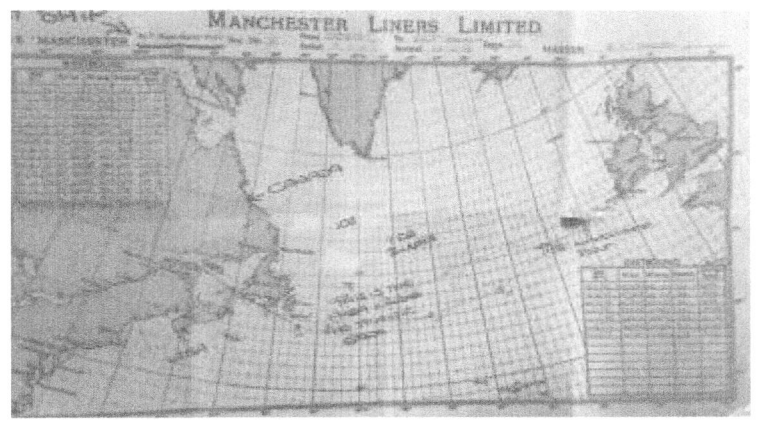

This chart shows the daily distance our ship was making while navigating across the North Atlantic outward bound. Then used again on the homeward-bound journey in nautical miles.

Some of the lads told me that we would most likely see icebergs as we approached the coast of Newfoundland. I wasn't sure if they were just having me on. Now we were well and truly on our way to our first port of Montréal in Canada. I was really excited about this and so was my cabin mate now the colour had returned back into his face.

After I had eaten breakfast, I just had time to look out of the porthole from the messroom and couldn't believe my eyes as there was this huge chunk of white ice on our port side. I was gobsmacked as I had only seen things like this in films. For once I managed to keep my breakfast down now that we had left the North Atlantic. I just had to have another look at these huge so-called 'growlers'. I could not help but think of the films I'd seen about the sinking of the *Titanic*. I recalled that this was the area where that beautiful ship had hit an iceberg that had sent the ship, along with most of the passengers, to the bottom of the ocean.

We sighted land on the starboard side and, looking ahead from the bow, I could see more huge icebergs in various shapes and sizes. They were floating along like driftwood, only a lot bigger. One of the sailors told me that two thirds of the icebergs were below the waterline so it was hard to imagine how big these monsters actually were. My happy moment was short lived. It was back to reality and the cruel treatment from the lads just continued throughout the voyage. My cabin mate and I just grew to accept that this was the way it would be until the day arrived for my promotion to able seaman.

It is common practice for any crew member to be labelled with a nickname if they stick out from the crowd or do something really stupid on the voyage. Well, I woke up one morning unable to open my left eye. It was all swollen and I couldn't understand why. This worried me, because being on the other side of the world, I couldn't exactly phone for a doctor's appointment. There was no trained medical staff onboard because we didn't carry any passengers, only crew. The only alternative was to go and see the Chief Steward, who was supposed to have some basic medical knowledge, if he was ever sober. Nevertheless, after looking my problem up in an out-of-date medical journal, he suggested that I had a stye in my eye. He applied some ointment to the affected area and told me to keep it covered up with an eye-patch. So that was it, when I reappeared back on deck to join the others, there was a huge burst of laughter. It wasn't too long before someone called me 'Nelson' after the British naval commander and national hero, Horatio Nelson who was famous for his naval victories against the French during the Napoleonic Wars. So that was it; this renamed my name for the duration of the voyage, and all the following trips on this ship. 'Alan' no longer...

I learnt navigational theory at the sea school. When a ship navigated tricky waters along the shipping lanes and channels that lead into ports around the world, a vessel needed to be guided along these waters by a pilot. The reason for this is that a pilot has local knowledge of the waters through sea lanes into harbours. The pilot would come aboard from a pilot boat which met the ship before navigating into the harbour. This was a very tricky and dangerous procedure. The small pilot craft had to move in close enough to the ship's side, so that a pilot ladder could be lowered down to the boat. The swell and the winds played havoc while trying to keep both the ship and the boat moving at the same speed and allow the pilot to climb the ladder onto the vessel. The pilot would then take over from the captain in the wheelhouse and give instructions both to the officers on duty and the helmsman, who was steering the ship. The skipper however, remained in overall charge of the vessel. During the long trip up the St Lawrence Seaway, the procedure was repeated several times because of the distance to our first port of Montreal. The ship sailed up the river whilst breaking through the thick chunks of ice and cutting a path. Cracking and crunching could be heard as the ice began to break up, only to reform again in our wake.

As we approached Port of Quebec to exchange pilots again, the scenery was breathtakingly beautiful. Only now did I wish I had been taught about the wider world and its history so I could appreciate the surroundings that we were encountering in this wonderful country (then again, if the teachers had no time for us poor kids, what chance did we have of any knowledge about anything, other than how to turn up for school in the first place?).

This was my first real sight of another country apart from my own. The snow-covered churches, houses and the Fairmont Le Chateau Frontenac (formerly and commonly referred to as the Château Frontenac), is an historic hotel located in Quebec City. The hotel is situated in Old Quebec, within the historic district's Upper Town. I first learnt from the crew that this part of Canada was French, and that historically, they didn't like the British. As a young lad at the time I didn't understand the enmity but have since learnt that it stems from the fact that Quebec was called 'New France' before 1763 i.e. the part of North America colonized by France. France was defeated in the Seven Years War and from 1763, France lost all its claims to Canada while Britain acquired Upper Canada as a British colony. As early as the 1820s, nationalists were campaigning for greater autonomy for French speaking Quebec within the British Empire and rebellions had to be put down by the army.

During my research in writing this book, I came across the reason why the Brits removed the French.

This Day in History: The British Defeat the French In Canada (1759)

'On this day in history, in 1759, the British achieve a great victory in Canada. As a result of this victory, the British are able to conquer Canada and eventually added it to their Empire. The Seven Years War was a global war between the French and the British for territory and control of trade routes. The French with their Indian allies had been involved in a brutal war with the British and American colonists, since 1756. The British under General James Wolfe, invaded Canada and in a brilliant maneuver, they scaled the cliffs over the city of Quebec. The French marched out of Quebec,

the capital of Canada or New France and advanced to meet Wolfe on the Plains of Abraham. This battle was to seal the fate of Canada. Wolfe's army was well supplied and well equipped. The French had been practically cut off from France for some time, because of the British navy's almost complete control of the sea. Wolfe achieved a dramatic victory, defeating the Marquis de Montcalm's French army on this day in history. Wolfe himself was fatally wounded during the battle, but he died knowing that he had won a great victory and that he had won Canada for Great Britain'.

After changing pilots once again, our ship was underway heading for our first port of Montreal. The voyage into this port would take us sixteen hours sailing time and I keenly anticipated my first shore leave. Maybe because of my eye patch, the bosun seemed to have taken a shine to me; I wasn't sure if that was a good thing or not! Our next duties were to unleash the deck cargo so that the Canadian stevedores could unload the freight, then empty the cargo holds.

I understood that we would be in Montreal for two days, so I was hoping that I could have a few hours off to take a look around. To do so, however, I would need some Canadian dollars. I could have a 'sub' (payment from my pay) if I had sufficient available funds from my wages, after deductions from the monthly payments that I sent home to my mam.

The task of deciding this was the job of the chief steward; he was the one who calculated our salaries. He would summon the crew to his cabin to discuss the matter and it was his duty to contact our shipping agent in Montreal to advise him how much Canadian currency the crew would require. This information was relayed by the 'sparkle' (radio officer) who would contact the agent by ship's radio. When we berthed the agent would be there with the funds, orders for the captain regarding our next sailing destination, and also specifications for cargo to be loaded onto our vessel. I didn't know what to expect when we reached Montreal and was always curious and asking excited questions. The weather was bitterly cold, and my dress code left much to be desired: thin blue worn-out jeans, a shirt that I still had from the sea school, a flimsy jumper and an old pair of shoes. These items were by no means adequate to cope with the harsh North American weather.

Early next morning, we were woken up by the watch on deck sailor banging on our cabin door.

'Come on let's have you!' he barked. 'Stations in twenty minutes, get your arses out of your pits.' I was that excited I jumped up from my bunk and hit my head on the deck-head pipes but this didn't bother me after spending seven days at sea and throwing up for most of them. This was my reward – Canada! I had no idea what to expect. I got dressed and made my way up to the messroom grabbing a piece of burnt toast and a mug of tea, then up to the fo'c'sle head to help the sailors with tying up the ship alongside the dock.

The mooring ropes were all frozen and as I tried to pick up the eye of the rope, it wouldn't bend. It was like picking up a piece of steel pipe: the icicles were clinging and snapping as we tried to uncoil the flexible man-made rope. It took three of us just to pass the end through the fairleads and down to the men on the quayside. Eventually we were able to get all the ropes ashore and the ship was secured to the posts on the dockside. Next job was to lower the gangway so that the pilot could go ashore, and the agent and dockers could come onboard to start unloading our cargo. As I stood on the frozen deck, I was shivering - every part of my skinny body was like a bag of bones. The dockers started to board the ship. They were talking amongst themselves and I liked their accents. Just like Americans, I thought. I had only ever heard accents like these when watching films. However, there were some I couldn't understand, so I asked one of the sailors. He replied that they were French-Canadians because Montreal was part of the Québec Province. I could not figure out what they were talking about, the nearest I had ever been to anything French was onions. When the day's work finally ended, it was time to nip up to the chief steward's cabin.

'Hi Nelson!' he laughed, 'do you want your sub?'

'Yes, please, Chief, how much can I have?'

'Fifty bucks is all that you are allowed, until you have worked some more overtime, then we will look at it again.'

He handed me the dollars, I flipped through the small wad of notes. Erm ... two ten dollar notes, five dollar bills and five singles. I had never heard the word 'bills' for notes but had picked it up from the movies. They certainly weren't like the bills we got through our letterbox at home - they didn't get paid. Wow! I felt rich.

'Don't spend it all at once young Nelson!' the Chief barked not unkindly.

'I won't, but I will try and buy my mam something, just don't know what.' By about seven that evening most of the lads had gone ashore to the local bars (amongst other places). But this wasn't possible for me and my cabin mate, because the drinking age in Canada was twenty-one. In 1968, and for the first time in my life, I set foot on foreign soil – I was only sixteen years old and truly an innocent abroad trying to take it all in. It was a world away from where I live back home.

Most ports around the world had what was known as 'Missions to Seamen', kind of like a local church, but non-denominational. The manager of these establishments would come aboard ship with leaflets and the offer of organised trips to various events, all free of charge. So, this was my one and only chance to have a look round this magnificent city. We were taken into the heart of down-town Montreal; it was breath-taking: all the supersized American cars, some of which had white-walled tyres. They were monsters compared to our little cars at home.

Wait till I tell my mates back home, they will be jealous, I thought. Neon lights illuminated the shops and bars and the place was buzzing. People were dressed in thick clothing, many of them in quilted ski suits, and knee-length boots; they looked like Eskimos. As they walked past me I could see the vapour of their breath in the cold, bitter night. As for me, I had to keep clenching my fists just to keep the circulation going. Our escort asked us if were hungry.

'Yes,' I muttered through chattering teeth.

'It's time you sampled our hotdogs and burgers,' he replied. He then pulled over and said, 'Out we go guys, it's time to see the sights.'

We walked towards a huge hotdog stand. People were queuing with children pestering their parents for their favourite food. When we got to the front of the queue, the man behind the counter asked us what we would like. I spoke first, in my quavering English accent.

'Hotdog please!'

'You wanna onions and ketchup?'

'Yes please…'

'How about some fries and a coke?'

'Erm yes, Sir.'

My knees were knocking together in the searing cold and as I kept on moving my feet to keep warm, the snow beneath my flimsy shoes crunched like broken glass. I was handed this enormous hotdog with onions seeping out of the sides, and oozing ketchup. It swamped both of my tiny, thin hands. Now I knew these 'bad boys' were for real and not just what I had seen in the movies. Our guide asked if we wanted to have a wander around town,

'Yes!' my cabin mate and I replied excitedly. Off we went leaving the hotdog stand with its fairground-like lights disappearing in our wake.

'Would anybody like to take a trip over to the river and explore Expo-67?' the guide asked us.

I wasn't sure what this Expo-67 thing was. However, just before I made a fool of myself, the escort explained to us that it was an international convention centre for countries around the world to showcase their inventions to the public. We cruised through security as our guide knew the guard, having visited with many seamen in the past.

'Wow,' I said to my mate, 'this place is huge, never seen anything like it. Come on guys let's take a look around and see what this place has got to offer.'

It was like Disneyland for grown-ups. There were exhibits from all over the world. The British contribution was like a gigantic dome, built with sections of mirrored glass glistening like huge diamonds, glowing in the cold winter's evening as the sun began to sink over the horizon.

The next morning it was nearly time to leave Montreal and set sail up the St Lawrence Seaway into the Great Lakes. This is what I had been looking forward to since we left Manchester. To transit the vast waters of the seaway, we had to first navigate the giant lock system. This procedure took us from sea level into fresh waters. I was told that the lakes were enormous and very clean, as the last mooring rope slipped from the fo'c'sle head and into the icy waters. The entrance to the seaway was only a short distance from the port of Montreal. The bosun told me that I had been given the role of 'Boom Boy' and explained,

'Nelson, it's a formality that the deck boys, forward and aft of the vessel, are sent ashore whilst transiting the seaway locks system. The reason for this is to tie the ship alongside the quays of the temporary holding area while waiting for the ship's turn to navigate the seaway.

'Yeh, sure bosun!' I replied confidently. Nevertheless, I was wary of what I might be in for.

As we neared the first lock, we had to steam slowly forward to let a ship go past that had just passed through the large lock gates. As we approached the giant wooden gates, we slowly manoeuvred into the central position of the lock. The area around the seaway had observation towers where the public could watch the ships as they negotiated their way through the locks. People waved at us as we slowly left the first lock. We navigated our way slowly towards lock two. The first mate received orders from the pilot via his radio that we would have to tie up on the wharf because there were ships awaiting their turn in the locks ahead. The bosun ordered the crew to swing out the boom. He beckoned me to go with the seaman and put on a life jacket, and prepare to be go ashore to put the ship's mooring ropes on the bollards on the quay.

Oh my god, this was it, I had to sit on this small wooden seat with a rope running through the middle of it, then the enormous boom would be swung out overboard with me hanging on for dear life. I would be lowered on to the quayside to put our mooring ropes on to the bollards so that we could await our turn to enter the second lock.

The order came from the first mate,

'Swing out the boom! We're going alongside of the jetty.'

Jim, one of the able seamen, told me to sit on the seat that was dangling from the boom pole, and hold on tight.

'Out you go Nelson!' he roared. He pushed out the long boom until it reached out over the quay and as it began to swing out, it was bending with my weight. I was terrified. I was so high up off the jetty, the ship wasn't even alongside yet. If I fell off this pole I would be squashed between the ship's side and the wall of the quay but I had to show that I wasn't scared, otherwise I would have been given yet another nickname for the rest of the voyage. I hit the jetty like a ton of bricks, then I had to run forward to catch the heaving line that was attached to the massive, heavy rope, pull it towards the bollard and slip it over so that the winch man on the fo'c'sle head could heave it tight. After this punishing exercise, I had to leg it towards the stern and do the same again with the ropes so that both ends of the ship were secured to the quayside.

It wasn't too long before we received the order to let go of all the ropes and proceed into the next lock. As the ship began to move away from the quay, I had to run towards it and reach out to grab the Jacob's ladder that was dangling over the side and climb up to the deck. This procedure continued until we had navigated all the locks and were in Lake Ontario.

> 'The Great Lakes are the largest surface freshwater systems on Earth and contain roughly 21 percent of the world water supply the names of the five Great Lakes are Lake Superior, Lake Michigan, Lake. 'Huron, Lake Erie and Lake Ontario.' The Great Lakes - https://en.m.wikipedia.org/wiki/Great_Lakes

I never expected anything like it, and it made the treacherous journey across the North Atlantic well worthwhile. Toronto was on the horizon, our first port on the lakes. We had only been sailing for around twelve hours but as we drew nearer. I could see its massive skyscrapers in the distance. I couldn't wait to get the gangway down onto the quay and step ashore. When all the ropes were ashore onto the jetty, we had to unleash some of the cargo so that the dockers could board and unload the freight. My flimsy clothing was starting to become a real problem. I literally could not stand still due to the corrosive/biting cold.

Again, a seamen's mission representative came to the messroom to introduce himself. He asked whether anybody was interested in a city tour which my cabin mate and I jumped at. It gave us the chance of a free ride in his whopping American Chevrolet ('Chevy'). I hit the shower then put on my wretched 'go-ashore' attire. As I climbed into the back seat of this monster car, I felt like the US President in a motorcade. Off we went along the quay and out onto the freeway. The skyscrapers were so massive I couldn't even see the tops of them when I looked through the windows.

Looking back at my childhood, and the way I was treated at school, I was almost glad I hadn't achieved the same grades in education like most of the other well-off kids, because I wouldn't have been here to see all of this. (Some things are meant to be.) After riding around the city for some time, our guide informed us that we had now entered Young Street, the longest street in Toronto. He explained there wasn't much time to show us any more of the city because he had to take other sailors off a Dutch ship to give them the same tour. But at least I'd had a chance to look at the sights, without spending any of my remaining dollars.

After departing Toronto, we had a short journey across the lake to Hamilton, another Canadian port. We didn't have much cargo, so it was a short stop. I learnt that Niagara Falls wasn't too far away and had only seen the falls on television but they looked awesome. I knew that if I was to see the Falls, it would have to be now and from this port as I would never get the opportunity again. I decided to have a chat with our chief steward, so I knocked on his cabin door.

'Oh, it's you Nelson – how are you kiddo?'

'I'm alright, Chief, thanks,' I replied nervously.

He looked at me with concern. 'How's your eye, Nelson?'

I touched the sore spot but felt it best to act brave.

'It's getting better, but the cold doesn't help!'

He chuckled and I cleared my throat nervously.

'Chief, is there any chance of going on a trip to see Niagara Falls?'

He pondered for what felt like a very long moment.

'Yes, but we aren't here very long, not much freight for this port, but I'll see what I can do.'

I bade him a polite 'goodbye' but inside I was exultant. Just as I had finished my lunch, he popped his head through the porthole, and shouted,

'Nelson, the man from the seamen's mission is on his way, he's going to take you and anyone else who wants to go to Niagara, so be ready as soon as!' WOW, Niagara Falls, unbelievable, wait until I tell my mates back home about this, I thought! I wished I could have afforded a camera; I could have made them really jealous. Even though this port was the nearest to the falls, it was still a long journey to actually reach them. As we drove around a sharp incline from the highway, I could see what looked like a cloud of mist.

'What's that?' I asked.

The driver leaned over and said, 'That my boy is the mist and damp water that comes off the falls!'

I was almost struck dumb with awe.

'Wow, you mean we are here?'

'We sure are,' he smiled.

Then as we drove down the ravine, it was there in all its glory. What a sight! Unbelievable.

'Oh my god, just look at it, where does all that water come from, and where does it go? I gabbled in excitement.

I wasn't sure whether Niagara Falls was one of the wonders of the world but it was certainly a great wonder to me. I made it my mission to find out how this great waterfall came into being. Our driver parked the vehicle in a parking lot near some gift shops, and I was the first to dart down to the viewing wall surrounding the falls. The Canadian (Ontario province) side of the Niagara River formed a natural border with New York State being on the other side.

As I looked down into the basin of the falls with the clean, crisp water cascading down onto the rapids of this giant waterway, there was a small sightseeing vessel cruising up towards the bow of our ship on this magnificent waterway.

The sightseers on the little boat were getting a soaking from the spray but they were all wearing waterproof clothing and red hats. But soon, we had to leave as our ship was due to sail in a few hours' time. This was one sight that would remain with me for the rest of my life. I wished that my family could have had the opportunity I had that day to see that amazing and breath-taking view.

We were a bit late getting back and as we boarded the ship, some of the sailors were already taking in the mooring ropes. I changed into my work clothes and took up my station on the fo'c'sle head. We singled up to just two mooring ropes, before the gangway was lifted back on board. The pilot stepped out onto the wing of the bridge, and gave the command to let go, forward and aft, through his radio. Our vessel slowly moved away from the quay and out into the lake.

We had now arrived at our next port of Cleveland, Ohio, USA my first time in the States. Wow what would my mates make of this? I was in America, the land of cowboys who burst into saloons and smashed bottles over each other's heads, then fell out onto the streets to continue their battles with a shoot-out. Or the Chicago of Al Capone battling with the Feds (I didn't know what Feds were until my dad enlightened me during a late night black and white film). Without a TV I wouldn't have known any history of America or anywhere else other than Wythenshawe, in my innocence of youth.

The sailing time from Hamilton to Cleveland was about 24 hours then we would be in Lake Erie another vast waterway. So there was ample time to grab some kip and reflect upon all the places I had visited in the last two days. Upon arrival just outside Cleveland harbour, we had to drop anchor because we were not allowed alongside until American customs and immigration had cleared the ship and all her crew, which was standard US practice. Even if it was the middle of the night, everybody would be woken up and had to muster in the messroom when Immigration boarded for the four to six-hour process before the ship was allowed to enter the port of Cleveland. Then it was onto Detroit in Michigan then on from there to Chicago, Illinois. These cities were amazing. Detroit ('Motor City') was and still is the home of the Ford motor company and their vehicles were lined up on the docks waiting to be loaded onto awaiting ships. I was looking down at the quayside from the top of the gangway when I saw a police officer patrolling the harbour. He was armed to the teeth with guns and ammunition and a huge Alsatian dog prowling alongside. I didn't know which looked the meanest: the cop or the dog, or both of them!

I was starting to realise what a great country the USA was. This was a steep learning curve for me, not least the cultural differences from back home. Chicago (the 'Windy City') is a huge city situated in Lake Michigan with canals running through its network of skyscrapers. Once again, the local seamen's mission escort gave us a guided tour around this magnificent place. This was around April 1968 and as we headed into downtown Chicago, our car became surrounded by rioters and demonstrators, who were protesting about civil rights for black citizens in Chicago. I recall our driver telling us about the riots the year before.

This is what he told us...

'In the long, hot summer of 1967, due to the 159 race riots that erupted across the States, it was Martin Luther King who started the Chicago Freedom Movement and the rioting still continues.'

At one point I was terrified as some rioters were looting shops, smashing windows and running haphazardly onto the streets with their loot. Some of them ran out towards our car as we cowered inside, petrified. The driver tried to steer the big Pontiac away from the crowds, but as he tried desperately to avoid them, two massive black guys hammered on our windows and pressed their faces against the glass. Their faces were distorted as they rocked the car from side-to-side. Our guide shouted at us to push the inside lock buttons. I had never experienced anything like this in my life before and am not sure I ever want to again, but one thing is certain - these people were very angry. We left Chicago at around midnight. The skyline was in our wake with the Sears Tower standing proudly in all its glory. But I was glad we had returned safely after our terrifying experience. We called at several ports on our homeward journey, back through the Welland Canal then onto the St Lawrence Seaway. We dropped off the last pilot just downriver from Quebec. I wasn't looking forward to crossing the North Atlantic again, now that my stomach had all but recovered from our outbound trip. But one thing was for sure, I wouldn't have swapped my first experience at sea for any other way of life.

After being at sea for about six days, we reached the Irish coast, then the coast of Anglesey where we contacted the pilot. In those pre-internet days, the only source of information about life back in the UK had been the radio, but because of the swell and motion of the ship, it always appeared to be distorted and breaking up. As we approached the coast, we were at last able to listen to BBC Radio Two. It was great to hear Jimmy Young's voice and at that moment I felt as though I was now back home.

As the pilot boat neared the side of our ship, the swell made it very difficult for the helmsman of the boat to hold his craft level against the ship's hull for the pilot to climb aboard. It was just a matter of getting the timing right so that the pilot could leap onto the ladder. This was always a very dangerous and hazardous procedure but after one last attempt, the pilot leapt onto the rungs of the ladder and climbed aboard. We then sailed towards the Liverpool Bar, which was the next point for changing pilots. Now we were heading for the Mersey and towards the first of the Manchester Ship Canal Eastham Locks. Waiting for us at this first quayside was a representative from Manchester Liners. His job was to calculate the earnings and deductions from our voyage, so that we could be paid off. This was also an opportunity for Customs and Excise to search the ship for contraband that may have been hidden or stashed somewhere on board.

Our tobacco allowance was two hundred cigarettes or fifty cigars, and one bottle of spirts (called a 'docking bottle'). These rules weren't always adhered to. There was always the opportunist who would try to hide quantities of fags or cigars. In the USA, tobacconist's cigars were cheap to buy; a box of King Edwards (commonly known in the States as a 'poor man's cigar') could be bought for as little as £5 for 50, then resold back home for around £50, a real incentive to break the rules. The customs officers had ample time to search the ship during the long journey on to Manchester. The ship's accommodation was lined with Formica panels which were easy to remove from the structure of the bulkheads. Access to the inner spaces and voids was easy and they could then be searched for any hidden contraband. When we finally docked in Salford it was just a matter of lowering down the mooring ropes, making them fast to the bollards on the quayside, and putting the gangway down, along with the safety net, which was to stop anybody falling in.

It was around 1800 hours when we finally finished our duties, now it was time to shower and get ashore. After six weeks away I just wanted to see my family again, tell them all about my first trip abroad, and see their faces when I gave them their gifts from America.

Several taxis appeared down on the dock, I jumped into the back seat of one, asking the driver to take me to my home address. I was happy, had a suntan, ('a bronzy' as we called it), money in my back pocket and about three weeks' paid leave. The cab pulled up to my house; I paid the cab driver and gave him a big tip. Wow, I felt wealthy. I was proud of myself. I was hoping that the neighbours would be peeping through their curtains, and see how well I looked. My time had finally come to show them that at least one of the Whittakers had done well for himself. As I hauled my worn, battered, heavy suitcases up our front path, I stopped about halfway to the front door, I could hear voices from inside the front room. It sounded like Beverly, my little sister, calling out to my mam.

'Mam, I think Alan's here, come on down, Mam. Hurry, he's at the front door, run, quick, let him in, I want to see him before I go to bed.'

I could hardly contain my excitement. Here I was after about six weeks away at sea, and everybody wanted to see me. For the first time in my life, I felt important.

The door opened, and there was my mam, all five foot and a few inches of her, looking frail and sad. Beverly was standing in front of her and holding onto Mam's apron to steady herself. She was skinny and blue in colour. I didn't know whether to cry or laugh so, I stepped inside the door and put my grubby suitcases down onto the carpet-less cold floor.

'Alan!' my mam cried, 'You look fantastic, just look at your suntan, let me have a big kiss!'

'Go on then, if you must, but don't put your sloppy gob on my new Canadian shirt! Talking of which, I've got prezzies for you both.'

'Oh, Alan,' cried Beverly, what have you bought me?'

'I've got you a little doll from Canada. It's a Native Indian doll, dressed in their traditional clothes, I know that you collect toys, so this is what I've got you.'

'Oh, Mam, look at this, It's gorgeous all the way from Canada. I'm so happy!'

'We've missed you,' said Mam. Have you missed us?'

'Yes, I have. I wrote you a letter, but I was told that the mail takes a long time to arrive here, so you might not have got it yet.'

'Yes, Alan, it came two days ago, I was worried about you. How was your first trip?'

'Mam it was great, I was very seasick for most of the voyage, so I didn't eat much. So hopefully, when I sail again in a couple of weeks, I should be okay now that I've experienced the worst.'

I knew that that remark wouldn't go down too well, but I just wanted to get it out of the way. The sea was my new life now, and I was going to make it my career.

By the end of my first day home, all of my family had welcomed my return. After a good night's sleep on dry land, I made sure that everybody had a gift from my first trip away, no matter how small they were. I was treated like a returning hero and for the first time, I had my own bedroom. Even though it was the box room, I still had it all to myself.

Next morning, I was woken up by my mam, who had made me a cuppa. My how things had changed since I was last at home, and working three jobs to help keep my brother and sisters! It was time to start showing off to my mates. Now that I had acquired the taste for beer whilst at sea, I thought that I would chance my luck and walk into my local pub the Black Boy. The legal drinking age was eighteen. The only implication for this would be that I would be barred from the pub, but it was a risk I was prepared to take to show off my tan in the pub up the road. I decided to dress in dungarees and a blue shirt with an open neck to expose my tan. At around 7pm that evening it was cold. As I walked into the saloon bar of the Black Boy, I felt nervous but excited. The sounds from the jukebox were belting out my favourite Beatles song, 'Love Me Do'. Girls were dancing while the boys were eyeing them up for a date, if they were lucky.

The place was packed. It was a Saturday night, and everybody was drinking and smoking; I couldn't see the bar for the murky haze - part and parcel of the pub atmosphere at the time. I thought that maybe the haze would work in my favour as nobody would be able to spot me being underage. The buxom barmaid asked me what I wanted to drink, and I just muttered,

'Pint of bitter, please.'

'Dimple or straight glass?' she asked with a big, knowing smile exposing her teeth which were nicotine-stained. Her hair was bleached and her dress sagged when she bent over the bar, exposing a rather ageing bosom.

'Errr straight glass, please.'

She pulled the pint and smacked it down on the bar. Froth and beer slopped down the side of my glass.

'Two bob *young* man please,' she said.

I drew out a fresh, brand new ten-pound note and gestured for her to have a drink herself. This she did with another broad smile. Now it was time to show off. I pulled out two, full, twenty packs of *Benson & Hedges King Size* from my pocket, and stacked them on top of each other on the bar. I lit one and after a few drags, stumped it out in the overflowing, unemptied ashtray then lit another. The man next to me, said,

'Are you loaded or what? You just stubbed out a full ciggie!'

'Yes, they only cost me two quid for a carton of two hundred.'

'Two quid!' he shouted. 'One packet of twenty 1/8d, and that's just for Woodbines.' Benson & Hedges Sovereign were 3/10d for 20.

I felt relaxed and a little cocky. Nobody asked me how old I was so I went there every night until I went back to sea. The music had stopped, so I asked the barmaid for a pound's worth of shillings to feed the machine. I felt like a movie star who was signing autographs.

Off I strolled to the jukebox clutching my pint. I could feel eyes boring into my back, weighing me up. I dropped coin after coin into the slot, then selected ten records at random. At that very moment, I felt as though I was winning the respect that the Whittakers had never had. At last I had overcome the stigma that was attached to me and my family: I was as equal as the next man.

By about 10.30pm, I decided that I had had enough to drink, so I scooped up my fags, and I left, swaying from side-to-side which made me feel as though I was back at sea. I was hungry so I called into the chippy on my way home. As I joined the queue of late-night drinkers eager for their supper, one of the serving ladies, beckoned me over.

'Alan, Alan Whittaker, is that you?'

'Yes, it's me, Mrs MacNeil.'

'You look terrific! Look at your suntan, and the clothes that you are wearing, you're all grown-up!'

'Yeah,' I replied in a preening manner, 'just got back from the States and Canada.'

'Wow, bet your mam is glad to see you.'

'Yeah, she is, and so is all my family.'

'Are you going back to sea then?'

'Oh yes, in a couple of weeks if my money lasts that long! Can I have pudding and chips with gravy in a tray? I've been longing for this moment for a good old chippy supper! I'd better take some chips home for my family so I'll have six portions of chips, and a large piece of cod for my mother. Hey, Mrs MacNeil, not on the slate anymore, ha-ha!'

She just smiled.

'...Oh, and plenty of salt and vinegar!'

As I approached our front door and reached out to knock, Mam opened it and I fell into the hallway, clutching onto our supper.

'Alan, are you *drunk*? Look at you! Get up and tek those chips into the kitchen. How much have you had to drink?'

'Not sure. Stop moaning, Mother, I've got you fish and chips. Should have seen everybody that knew me in the pub, Mam. They were all jealous of me spending my money like it was going out of fashion. It's our turn now, Mam, after all the years that we had to put up with everybody looking down at us. From now on life will be a lot better for us all, sod the lot of them.'

I suddenly noticed that my sister wasn't there.

'Where's Bev?' I asked.

'She's in bed, she wanted to stay up and see you, but you know how tired she gets.'

'Yes, Mam, I know. I thought about her a lot while I was away at sea, but maybe one day she will get better.'

'So, when do you intend to go back to sea?'

'In about two weeks, if my money holds out.'

'How long for this time?'

'I will be signing on the same ship, so it will be about a six-week trip again, same ports as last time.'

There was no reply, just silence while we all got stuck into our chippy supper. As the days passed my pay disappeared quicker than I expected, so I had to ease up on my nights out in the Blacky.

The day soon arrived when I had to pack my bags and head to Manchester Liner's office at Salford Docks, to sign on for my second voyage. I didn't want to make a fuss about leaving, so I just went and waved goodbye to everybody as they peered through our cracked, stained windows. I didn't bother with an ostentatious taxi and just caught a bus.

Voyage two on the *Manchester Port* was pretty much the same as the first, even down to the racking sea sickness. I eventually completed four voyages as a deck boy on the vessel. Trip three was not as good. I was summoned to the captain's cabin by the first officer as we sailed up the St Lawrence River in Canada. I could tell by the look on his face that something was wrong, and he maintained an uncomfortable silence on the way to the captain's room. The skipper informed me that he had received some bad news from home via a telegram. My youngest sister, Beverley, had passed away because of a hole in her heart at the age of seven. The captain would not let me fly home because, he informed me, there were 'other members of my family to grieve' for my sister. My heart was broken. As I was 'only' a deck boy, my duties for the rest of the voyage could have easily been reallocated. It was then that class distinctions hit me. If it had been one of the officers, they would have been on the next plane home. The remainder of that voyage was tough. So, I just kept myself to myself. Most of the crew were very sympathetic, which helped ease the pain a little. My elder brother, Arthur, who had been granted leave to fly home for my sister's funeral, couldn't understand why I was not allowed the compassionate leave that he had been granted. Not being able to see my sister for one last time had only added to my heartache and grief. To this day, I feel anger and hatred towards that captain for his lack of empathy and sensitivity. There is a saying that we can forgive but not forget. I can't do either towards that man.

After completing my fourth and final voyage on the *Manchester Port*, it was time to move on and leave *Manchester Liners* to broaden my travels to other parts of the world. My next adventure was on a coaster, a smaller vessel that only sailed around the UK coast. The *Aberthaw Fisher* was built in 1966 at the Ailsa Ship Building Company, Glasgow and was originally used for transporting heavy loads to the new generation of power stations being built around Britain; hence its roll-on, roll-off capability. The motorway network systems weren't as extensive in the 1960s. So, it was more efficient to use coastal vessels that transported by road.

I joined the *Aberthaw Fisher* at Pomona Docks, an extension of Salford Docks, and which were the original docks of one, two, three and four). The berth for my ship and its sister ship the *Kingsnorth Fisher* was specially adapted to allow these two ships to tie up stern first like a giant ramp, so that the huge trucks could manoeuvre onto the ship transformers and offload their cargo. Whilst serving on this ship, I gained my first promotion to Senior Ordinary Seaman (SOS). This qualified me to gain my steering certificate (steering ticket) so I was now able to work on the watch keeping system.

Normally, the skipper is the boss on a vessel. But on this ship, it was the chief cook! He ruled the roost (not the waves) and whatever went on during the voyage, or even in port, he knew about it. Then he would make sure the 'old man' got to know. When the ship was tied up in port, there had to be a seaman on night watchman duties. The procedure to decide who would get this 'cushy number' was to cut the cards and whoever turned over the highest card would get the role. This came with perks, such as four hours overtime on weekdays and twelve hours overtime at weekends. The duties of the night watchman ensured the safety and welfare of the ship and crew and entailed patrolling the entire ship throughout the shift. Along with that came the waking of all the crew in the morning. However, if for any reason the stewards and cook failed to be called, there was hell to pay. After cutting the cards, lady luck came my way and I turned over an ace. The watchman's working shift was from 1900 to 0700. Each evening, when I had done my rounds, I would make a point of making regular appearances round the galley to ensure that the cook had seen me. I also patrolled around the officers' accommodation to check that all was quiet and the moorings were secure.

I looked around to see if there was anybody about, and so as not to arouse suspicion, I made a beeline down the gangway to the dock gate, then walked towards the bus stop to wait for the bus to Wythenshawe to see my family and spend a few hours in the *Blacky*. I was basically getting paid for having a good time in the pub! Some nights I would wander home at closing time, visit the chippy, get my head down for a few hours, set my alarm to 0400 hours, then catch the first bus back to the Pomona Dock. If I had failed to get back onboard before anybody noticed me missing, or worse still, if I had not arrived back in time to call the cook and the stewards, I could have been up before the old man, and kicked off the ship. My antics continued until the ship left Pomona, without anybody being any the wiser, not to mention all the overtime that I had claimed. Sailing round the UK coast wasn't very exciting, and we were constantly sailing through bad weather. One thing was for sure: I had overcome my seasickness problems! After completing my time on this ship, it was time to really venture to other parts of the world.

In 1969, my brother Arthur and I had a so-called 'work-bye' (temporary work) on one of the *Port Lines* cargo ships at London's King George Docks while waiting with other crew members to fly out to Philadelphia for a five-month (but they trips were always longer than we are told) trip aboard the *Port Montreal*. It was standard procedure to join ships abroad and this was known as a 'fly-out job'. That was because most shipping companies had their trading contracts overseas. It was consequently more cost-effective and less time-wasting to charter flights with a full crew than to fly them out individually by commercial flights. It was during this period that some crew and officers were together for the first time. It was like having a drunken football supporters' bus returning home after winning the World Cup. Alcohol was in abundance and the abuse that was given to the stewards was undeserved and uncalled for.

The night before we were due to fly out to the States, we hit the local bars to have a few bevvies before leaving the UK. The next morning, most of us surfaced from our cabins sporting very sore heads. But a few hours later, we were loaded into a coach to take us to Heathrow, where we were joined by the officers and the rest of the crew. After being informed that our flight was running about four hours late, we were (yes, you guessed it) off to the bar again. After about three hours we all regrouped at the check-in desk. In those days, there were no terrorist problems for the security staff. Most of us were a bit worse for wear and boisterous. One seaman, in particular, decided to provide us all with some entertainment with his break-dancing routine, but he keeled over only to stagger back to his feet with a big shiner on his left eye. This behaviour did not go down very well with the skipper. Once onboard the aircraft, it was a non-stop piss-up and the language was beyond anything that I had heard before. The poor old stewardesses just had to grin and bear it and hope that everybody would have had enough and just flake out.

Upon our arrival in Philadelphia, we were taken to the Benjamin Franklin five-star hotel. It was not the sort of hotel that seamen were accustomed to staying at whilst waiting to join a ship. It had a degree of luxury that was totally unexpected. The crew was put in one room while the officers were put in another - big mistake! We were accustomed to staying at one to two-star hotels, which were more like brothels, whilst waiting to join a ship.

I asked one of my fellow crewmates, Trevor Bodiam, who I had tracked down after 50 years through The British Merchant Navy Old Friends Club (more about Trevor later in this story) to help me fill in the gaps of my memories.

He said that he remembers the young black pageboys in the hotel lobby who were dressed like servants in the *Gone with the Wind* era: red jackets with breeches and stockings. He also recalled somebody ordering cold beers and when asked who was paying, the reply was, 'Just put it on the tab!' As he noted, this was just to see if we could get away with it before ordering anything else. Then we were all ushered into a stately room. To our surprise, there was a knock on the door and in walked the waiters with a tray full of cold beers and a slip of paper showing the amount to be charged to our room. That was it - no money required. Now it was time to party. I do not remember who picked up the phone next to request some more beer, gin and some steaks and French fries. But the service was relentless. It reminded me of the kid in the Home Alone film ordering huge amounts of pizzas and ice cream and charging it to his dad's credit card. It must have been about five hours before we were asked to vacate the room and make our way down the hall to the front entrance to board our bus to the docks. We never knew who footed the final bill, but it wasn't any of us, so it must have been paid by the shipping agent.

At the time, I was a young naïve deck boy who didn't know what he was in for. On climbing up the gangway of the *Port Montreal* it looked enormous compared to the *Manchester Port*. Soon after we boarded, we were mustered in the messroom and the chief mate decided to upset everybody before we had even set sail from our first port. He announced that it was his job to cut overtime costs and keep any necessary overtime to a minimum. Wow, that was a huge blow to us; a seaman's wage wasn't much to begin with. Overtime was vital to allow small but necessary luxuries such as tobacco, alcohol and subs for going ashore, not to mention sending an 'allotment' (monies) home to our families. So, morale was at rock bottom from the start, and his announcement proved to be a BIG mistake on his part; it would later come back to haunt him. The night before we set sail to our second port on the eastern seaboard most of the lads went 'up the road' (ashore) and pooled their available dollars. I could not go because of the strict American drinking laws.

The next morning, most of the crew - ABs, stokers and the catering department - all appeared topside nursing bad heads. We left Philly that morning, only to discover that my brother, Arthur, and another lad were not amongst the crew. They had apparently got drunk and missed the ship. They were reunited with us at Boston, our next port. This was the start of one hell of a voyage for them. They had to repay all the incurred expenses relating to their absence, so they were already in debt to the ship before earning even a day's pay

I shared a cabin with a senior ordinary seaman (SOS), also commonly known as an 'ordinary tab-nab' ('tab-nabs' are biscuits or cakes). My rating was one step lower, junior ordinary seaman (JOS). His SOS ranking gave him seniority over me, so he chose the bottom bunk and I was banished to the top. Junior seamen, catering staff and deck boys all had to share whilst engine room ratings and all other seamen enjoyed single berth cabins.

Only British Merchant ships carried alcohol. It had to be purchased from the chief steward, usually at a set time of day, and signed for on our tabs. It was traditionally consumed in someone's cabin, but on this ship, we were fortunate to have a crew bar. This was situated at the aft end of the ship on the poop deck. This was an ideal location for us, as it was away from the officers' accommodation. It was well fitted out with all the standard amenities of any shore-side bar, but also had a record player and multi-coloured disco lighting.

The *Port Montreal* was designed to carry dairy and meat products from Australia and New Zealand, but also general cargo from other destinations, including the USA. After we left Boston, we continued down the east coast visiting coastal ports before sailing through the Panama Canal, which links the Atlantic and Pacific Oceans. This was a mind-blowing experience for we younger lads who had not experienced it before. The climate was now tropical, so the atmosphere was very hot and humid.

The Panama Canal was built and operated by the US Government. It had a different lock system from the Seaway that led to the Great Lakes. Locomotives pulled the ships transiting through the massive locks. Bulky wire ropes were secured by pulleys onto the locos and then tensioned up to compensate for the rapid rise or descent in the water chambers that were used to lower or lift vessels up to the level of the waterways. Sometime before we arrived at the canal the lads would ask us (the rookies) to go to the galley and ask the cook for some bread to feed the mules. Apparently, 'the mule' reference was because ships were pulled by these beasts before the locomotives replaced them. I, for one, did not fall for that feeding the mule trick, but the galley boy did!

The Americans finished it as a lock canal. It opened in 1914 and 3.4 million cubic meters of concrete went into building the locks. Nearly 240 million cubic yards of rock and dirt were excavated during the American construction phase. Of the 56,000 workers employed between 1904 and 1913, roughly 5,600 were reportedly killed. Dubbed one of the Seven Wonders of the Modern World by the America Society of Civil Engineers.

Ships transiting from the Atlantic Ocean side travel through three locks. Gatun is the first lock, which lifts the ships up about 26 meters. Once the ship is lifted up, it is then in the Gatun Lake freshwater lake, which provides the water to the lock chambers allowing the ships to be lifted up or lowered down. The second lake, Pedro Miguel locks, leads into the Miraflores Lake and Miraflores lock, which is the gateway to the Pacific Ocean.

These pictures are royalty-free from Pixabay.com

This was much better than my voyages across the Atlantic, and the sea was mostly calm and tranquil. I gazed at the stars above with no compunction to throw up over the side. There were many sightings of whales and dolphins, even flying fish that would kamikaze onto the decks. Most of the sailors were put onto day work shifts, leaving just one man on a watch. This was common practice so that more could be done on our three-week crossing and when we reached the Aussie coast, a two-man watch-would be implemented.

I am not sure how I got an unpaid and unqualified job as the Bosun's mate (commonly known as 'Lamp-trimmer' or 'Lampy'). I must have impressed somebody! I grabbed the unexpected opportunity, but I don't think the other ordinary seamen were very impressed. My primary duties were to prepare all the equipment, such as paints, maintenance equipment and 'soogeeing' gear (cleaning utilities). This was very much a Merchant Navy term. I believe that the word 'Suji', but pronounced by British sailors as 'Soogee' comes from the Hindi *'sujimutti'* meaning 'caustic earth' as well as anything else the sailors needed to carry out their daily duties. This was a good number for me, as I didn't have to work as much as the rest. (I quite liked being a teacher's pet!).

Most of the time we just wore shorts and T-shirts. There wasn't even much 'dhobying' (laundry) to be done. Because it was so hot, I just put my clothes out to dry on top of one of the cargo hatches. Most of the time my skin would be burnt red which kept me awake at night. There was no such thing as sun-cream and even if there had been, we would have been called 'pansies' had we used it. Even worse, after finishing maintenance duties, we used neat turpentine to clean paint off our hands, which was quite corrosive and drying. It is a miracle that I escaped any long-term skin issues.

It was on the *Port Montreal* that I experienced the 'Crossing the Equator' or 'Line Crossing' ritual. Although the ceremony is around 400 years old, even in antiquity, sailors engaged in rituals when passing certain parallels. Traditionally, it marks a sailor's first crossing of the Equator and initiates them as a 'Son of Neptune'. When we reached this point, it was an onboard tradition to have certain rituals performed such as having the initiates' hair shaved off or drenching them with raw eggs and custard, flour and anything else that the cook had left over from the day before.

In more recent times, events were captured on a Polaroid camera as evidence, and on this occasion, there were four of us mortals who hadn't crossed the line before. Having my elder brother on board meant that there was no escaping my fate, and needless to say, there was nowhere to run on a cargo liner. I just lay there and accepted my punishment.

There was always something to liven up the crossings. Once, somewhere in the middle of the Pacific Ocean, we decided have a mock 'wedding ceremony'. My brother Arthur 'married' one of the gay stewards. In those more innocent days, there was no homoerotic or homophobic undertones to this; it was just done for a laugh before we hit the Australian coast.

I was to be the best man. The bride's wedding outfit and the groom's suit were made from old, spare sailors' clothes. The bride's blonde wig was made from old man-made rope. Even the wedding rings were made from pieces of wire. The ceremony was held in the crew's bar, and we even made fake telegrams that would have been sent from their families, wishing them all the best. The chippy (carpenter) had an accordion, and he played the wedding song, 'Here Comes the Bride' as the happy couple entered the bar to gales of raucous laughter and song. To date, I have never seen any photographs of this event which is just as well as my brother wouldn't want to see them! (There were pictures taken.) To date, there is no official record of their 'registration' of marriage. It would have been great to have some record of this amusing ceremony, just for laughs in the pub back home.

I hope that my brother Arthur reads this book one day. He will remember that it was just staged for a bit of fun and nothing more.

After three weeks at sea, the Australian coast was on the horizon - a beautiful sight. Our onboard bar attracted people from ashore to come on board and have one or two beers. The girls especially were a much welcome sight, however, coming aboard was not all that they did. They would invite us ashore to parties, and we would go to the world-renowned Monty's Bar in Sydney's harbour. Unfortunately for me and the other first trippers with our heads shaved off like sheep after sheering time, we weren't a very attractive sight, so we could only watch in envy of the other guys. The seamen would be drinking like it was going out of fashion. Inevitably, before the night was out, the brawling would start. It was like something out of a Western: jugs of beer, glasses and cans - you name it, were thrown around the bar. At curfew time, we would stagger back to the ship, girls in tow! This ritual would be the same in every port, day-in-day-out. The tricky part was trying to emerge in the morning and put in a day's work - if that's what you would call it. The bosun would hammer on our cabin doors at seven in the morning; all you could hear along the alleyways was, 'bugger off!'. I blearily wondered how I had got back onboard and how come I was still fully clothed. On many occasions, the morning trip to the bathroom for a shower would be an eye-opener in more ways than one. Some of the girls who had decided to stay the night would just parade around in their underwear. Believe me, it was a sight for sore eyes. This was definitely not what I had expected from my maritime career (it wasn't mentioned in the brochures!). It was complete madness, but I was glad to be a part of it...

One of the girls, Hendrix (real name Jill Steinberger), took some of us to her parents' house up in Sydney's Blue Mountains.

(Top Left) Peter Ryder (used with his permission). [Right] 'Hendrix' (Jill Steinberger) & friends in Monty's Sydney (used with permission) ©2020 Alan Whittaker

By the time the trip was at the halfway mark, we were losing crew members as some had jumped ship. There were times when we left port that someone would still be ashore in some rundown bar or brothel. By the time we were due to leave the Australian coast and return back to the USA, there must have been one-third of the crew missing. The AB (who keeled over at the airport) was working inside one of the cargo hatches and discovered barrels of unfermented red wine down there. He discovered that he could tap into one of the barrels without any leakage and decided to try a tipple of this Aussie nectar. How much he consumed is anybody's guess. It later transpired that he was a hopeless alcoholic. One night there was a commotion heard from his cabin when we were in Melbourne. When a crew member entered, he discovered the sailor having a fit, so an ambulance was called. He was given the once-over and stretchered off the ship to the local hospital. Later, it was discovered that he was suffering from the DTs. (*delirium tremens*) this is referred to as symptoms ranging from mild to severe withdrawals from alcohol.

He didn't return to the vessel and we were led to believe that after having some treatment in the hospital, he was flown home as a DBS (Disabled British Seaman (more like 'Drunken British Seaman!) The voyage back to the States took around three weeks, so that gave everybody time to recuperate and recharge their batteries, ready for the forthcoming assault on the American coast. By this time, most of us were fairly broke, so it was a matter of whoever could get a sub (loan) from their salary would pay for everything until someone else could pick up some cash. That's how it was.

Each time we left a port, American girls would drive to the next one to meet up with our ship as she docked. We sailed down the eastern coast of the United States which lasted about a month, then it was back through the Panama Canal and into the Pacific Ocean on our way over to Australia. This was to be our second and last visit to Aussie before we left for home. Our first port of call was Sydney and we were looking forward to going ashore because most of the crew had made many friends on our previous visit. I remember arriving in Sydney at about midday, and we were informed that there wasn't a berth (a place in the docks) available for our ship until the next morning, so we lay at anchor until first thing the following day. The weather was fantastic. Most of the crew was drinking in the bar again which was located at the stern of the ship. After a couple of hours, we noticed a small canoe with two young lads circling the stern of the vessel. They were waving at us and shouting, 'Would you like us to take you ashore?' This was not what you would expect to hear so believe it or not, one of the seamen came to the stern armed with a pilot's ladder and over it went. He decided to make his way down to the canoe, followed by many more of the lads. It was an unbelievable sight. The boys took them ashore and then returned to pick up some more; it was like a shuttle service. When darkness fell, I could hear laughter coming from down below in the water; everybody was returning back on the same boat in which they went ashore.

Most of them were the worse for wear and having great difficulty in climbing the ladder. The next morning, the pilot boarded our ship to take us into port. The captain, unaware of our antics, had trouble trying to figure out why some of the crew were already waiting on the quayside! (He was told about them later.) As soon as we were alongside, the skipper ordered the missing sailors up to his cabin and when he was informed of the canoe incident, all hell broke loose. All the missing crew were fined five days' pay with some of their leave withdrawn. After leaving Sydney, we called at four more ports along the coast until we arrived in Freemantle, Western Australia, which was our last port before sailing home.

We should have only been in this port for a couple of hours. Almost the entire crew had illicitly gone ashore after being told that there was no shore leave. We all just headed for the well-known watering hole Cleo's. At the end of the day, some of the officers had to leave the ship and go searching all the local bars to round up the motley crew and put them in taxis to return to the vessel.

Once onboard, most of us crawled into our cabins and flaked out. The next day, when we all surfaced, the ship was at sea. The trip lasted for about ten months and by then, the ship was down to about half of its original crew. My brother, Arthur, decided to leave the ship in Australia to avoid any repercussions if he stayed on the ship. When the vessel arrived back in London we were paid off, but this wasn't any ordinary signing off procedure, which would only take around one hour. It lasted about most of the day because the master and first mate wanted to punish the older ratings for their rampant misbehaviour throughout the voyage. I suppose it would be fair to say that the skipper had the last laugh. The ABs and the engine room ratings were given double DRs (declined to report), which was recorded in their discharge books. This meant that each individual had to go before a committee to explain their bad behaviour. It also meant that they could be struck off the shipping federation register and wouldn't be allowed to return to sea. This was an extreme but effective punishment. After signing off, we said our goodbyes. It was sad because I felt as though I was leaving part of my family behind.

I only spent a short leave at home because I didn't pay off with much money after the antics on the *Port Montreal*. It was time to go to the shipping federation in Salford to look for another ship. Upon arrival at the 'Poole' (shipping federation), I scanned the white vacancy board on the back wall. There didn't seem too much in the way of deep-sea jobs on offer apart from a couple on *Manchester Liners,* and I wanted to give them a miss for a while. So, after getting clearance from the Poole officer, I got a temporary transfer and went down to London's Poole (acceptable if there weren't any vacancies in our home port). In London, I was offered a ship from the *Blue Star Line*, which was another fly-out job to Cape Town. I had to wait for a couple of days before I could fly out to join the ship with the rest of the crew, so I worked on the *English Star* to earn a few quid to keep me going. On 22nd of April 1970, our chartered plane arrived in Cape Town. The difference this time was that we weren't ensconced in a plush hotel whilst waiting to board the ship. We were driven by coach straight from the airport down to the docks. This ship, the *Newcastle Star,* would visit several ports around the southern peninsula of the southern coast of South Africa, then it was about a twelve-day crossing through the Indian Ocean on to Australia. My rating for this voyage was Senior Ordinary Seaman, a small step towards EDH (Efficient Deck Hand) status. Once we had found our way around the ship and offloaded our bags into our cabins, we exchanged some sterling for Rands (their currency). After this (yes, you guessed it!) up the road we went to get acquainted with one another. However, there weren't many local bars open, only nightclubs. Having already consumed a few bevvies in the airport, it didn't take much for us to get pissed.

The next morning our 'Peggy' (mess-man) was reported missing. He was a six-foot, well-built Geordie and about forty-five years old, which was unusual for a Peggy. It was normally a young boy's role on his way up the promotional ladder in the catering department. Later that day, he came aboard looking like a bus had just hit him. He was wearing a dark suit and white shirt and tie, which were covered in bloodstains. He had to report to the chief steward and explain why he had not shown up for work that morning. He had been drinking all night and decided to meet up with a black lady. South African apartheid laws of the time forbade fraternisation or relationships with black folk. I wasn't sure what apartheid meant until one of the lads who had frequently visited South Africa explained to me that black and white individuals or people were forbidden by law to integrate. Whites walked on one side of the street, while blacks walked on the other. The same rule applied to buses, trains and any other form of transport, along with shops, bars and restaurants. I found this very difficult to understand; whites ruled and that was that. We later learned that the mess man and his lady friend had been picked up by the 'Yarpies' (Dutch Police). They were taken to the police station and put in a cell. Both had been beaten. We also learned from the steward that the Yarpies had beaten the woman as brutally as they had our Peggie. The mess man was taken to court that day and received a heavy fine. This incident didn't go down very well with the chief steward. I'm not sure if the mess man received any more punishment from the skipper.

He hadn't been the only one as two of the ABs also went ashore one night and hooked up with two black women, only this time they went a stage further and brought the women back to the ship. I wasn't aware of this until the next morning when the two sailors sobered up, only to realise what a big mistake they had made. Not only had they broken the law by fraternising with black women, but they had to get them both ashore in broad daylight without the Dutch police seeing them. Somebody suggested that disembarkation could be possible if the women were dressed like stevedores, so the two sailors raided the oil-skin locker and found some old boiler-suits and some sea-boots (wellingtons). After dressing up the women and putting some dirt on their faces, they were told to make their way down the gangway onto the quay and told to speak to no one. This must have worked because they were never heard of or seen again. If the police had apprehended them, they would have been made to identify the two men on the ship and all hell would have broken loose.

The situation in South Africa was a real eye-opener for me. Where I was born in Wythenshawe, South Manchester, we were all equal. Only about five miles away from my home was Moss-Side with a large black, mixed-race and African community. We were all brothers and sisters who lived and worked together in harmony. The only distinction that I grew up with was class distinction. South Africa reminded me of the 1988 film *Mississippi Burning*, that portrayed the 1960s racism and hatred of the southern states of America.

I experienced the fallout from such prejudice and injustice via the American 'Jim Crow' laws that Luther King did so much to try and abolish. The race riots that were seen in America were all part of this. Drugs and drug trafficking have long been an issue onboard ship. When I was on the *Port Montreal*, I knew a couple of guys who were civilians from shoreside in Australia and were always asking for cannabis.

Then when we visited the Aussie coast again on the *Newcastle Star*. It wasn't very long before they came onboard asking for some weed. They would offer large sums of money for a small amount of grass. At that time, it was an offer that some of the lads just couldn't refuse. These buyers would offer 100 dollars just for information on how or who had grass to sell. They were dealers, although in those days, we did not realise that. I had very little experience of the drug world and didn't realise they were dealers. It surprised me as Australia is the ideal place to grow it!

When we returned to South Africa for the second leg of on the *Newcastle Star,* some of the black stevedores would approach the sailors whilst working on deck. The ones that could speak a little English would ask the lads if they were interested in cannabis, in exchange for South African currency. This would have provided the dockers with much-needed revenue to support their families who most likely would be living somewhere in the townships, and to supplement their poor wages. It goes without saying that they would have been punished for their crimes. Drinking was always accepted on British merchant ships, but not marijuana. It was also a known fact that smoking pot made a person's mouth very dry. So, to overcome this, soft drinks were purchased from the 'bond in bulk' (cases) as drinking alcohol would have defeated the object of getting 'high'. After negotiations and some bartering, money would be exchanged for large quantities of cannabis, which was concealed in brown paper bags camouflaged in old rags. Most of the ship's crew were young guys, so many of the ABs were into smoking weed. The problem was concealing the pungent smell from anybody passing the cabins so the guys used masking tape to seal around the internal cracks on the cabin doors and this worked well until the doors were opened, then (as the song goes) 'smoke gets in your eyes'.

I think the captain must have thought what a great crew he had on board seeing as they were mostly so well behaved and didn't drink. Little did he know that when the ship was sailing across the Indian Ocean most of the lads were higher than the stars above!

After paying off the *Newcastle Star,* I signed on to the Federal Steam Navigation Co. ship *S.S. Devon* which was berthed at London's King George the IV dock. This four-month voyage was to be the last one before it went to scrap or 'cut up for razor blades' as we called it. As this was her last voyage, there was a very relaxed atmosphere, and there wasn't much maintenance to be done on a ship that was due to be broken up. We exported cargo to New Zealand via the Panama Canal. We had a short stay in Panama and took on some 'bunkers' (fuel) as we were due to sail to New Zealand. It was swelteringly hot, so as my watch mate and I were off duty we decided to go up the road (ashore) for a few cold ones, wearing just shorts and flip-flops. We seemed to lose track of time and drank too much, and when we got back, the ship was ready for sailing. We were late for our duties and assisting with bringing in the gangway and letting go of the mooring ropes. The bosun told us to go down below and sleep it off. The next morning, however, we were summoned to the skipper's room and received a fine of three days' pay (a 'logging') and that was the end of it. We wouldn't have got off so lightly if the ship had not been on her last voyage.

The *S.S. Devon* was carrying six racehorses. They were stabled in purpose-built horseboxes, secured down on the deck. A dedicated onboard groom fed and looked after them, but it was our job to open the cargo hatches and lift out the straw and hay. As we neared the coast of New Zealand, the horses sensed the approaching land and became restless, kicking out in their boxes. Livestock, including horses, are transported by sea to this day.

We visited several ports on the Kiwi, one of them was at the southern end of the South Island Bluff. Once alongside, two women came aboard our ship. One of them had blonde hair and was very pretty. She was introduced as 'Diane'. The lads and these two girls were chatting and drinking beer, when my eye caught Diane's. It wasn't too long before we both rearranged our seats and sat next to each other. I couldn't believe my luck. The bar was packed with good-looking, horny seamen, but she chose me. She even tried to keep me on the straight and narrow. By this I mean sobering up a little because she told me later that when she first entered our bar, she spotted me on the couch, out cold from too much drink. Even today, I wonder what would have happened if I had jumped ship for her; I could have made a new life in New Zealand. She even bought me a Paul McCartney album because she knew I was a Beatles fan. En route back to the UK, we stopped off at Panama again. When we arrived there, to my surprise, I was handed a letter from Diane! This was really unexpected but a lovely thought. After that and once we left for home, however, I sadly never heard from her again.

The M.V. Majestic Shaw Saville was my next job.

Another fly-out job to Piraeus (Greece) on 13th April 1971. (Thirteen was never my lucky number!) I signed on as an Efficient Deck Hand for the five-month voyage. The skipper on this vessel was renowned for logging anybody who stepped out of line and was notorious on the Kiwi coast for being a bastard and banning girls from coming onboard. This was in total contrast to the relaxed atmosphere of the *Devon*, where one would have to do something really bad to get logged. We sailed from Piraeus through the straights of the Bosporus into the Black Sea. We then headed for Odessa, then part of the Soviet Union. The reality of life behind the Iron Curtain was a mystery to me, and I was in for a big culture shock. As we sailed into the harbour, Soviet naval ships followed us. After we had docked, we were informed that we weren't allowed ashore without our ID cards. At each end of the vessel and at the bottom of the gangway, guards toting Kalashnikov AK 47 rifles stood motionlessly. They looked more like statues than humans and never flinched or moved. On the other side of the harbour, there seemed to be huge timber logs lined up next to each other in the water. I was later informed that they were submarines captured from the Germans after WWII and just left to rot.

I was sent to see a doctor whilst we were in Odessa an unforgettable experience. The exterior and interior of the hospital was very old and the equipment seemed about twenty years behind the West. Some of the doctors and nursing staff were big buxom women. They looked more like all in wrestlers and not what Westerners would expect in the hospital service. En route in a taxi, I looked at goods displayed in the Odessa shop windows. Furniture, TVs, and electrical goods all looked dated and behind the times.

People walking along the streets did not look happy, and their fashion sense left something to be desired. I do recall walking up the 155-yard steps of Odessa ('Potemkin') Stairs, the famous entrance to the city from the sea. It is not something they do out of politeness, so it is easy to misinterpret the glum faces. I also found it odd when I went past ordinary stores queueing for what seemed just basic foodstuffs. The cab driver could speak a little English and told me that when the ladies were shopping at the markets they were not allowed to speak to one another, but he didn't reply when I asked him why not.

When we finally left Odessa for the Black Sea, Soviet warships shadowed us until we were clear of the port. I noticed that the Also Russians found it odd and even insincere that we smile and grin at every opportunity.

These pictures are copyright free. The hospital is called Odessa Regional Clinical Center (Former Odessa Seafarers Hospital). Located on 1, Sudostroitelnaya Street, Odessa. Primorsky District. 15 minutes' drive from Odessa Port. Supplied by Natasha Dyba 2020

When we reached the Panama Canal, we had to wait for the pilot to navigate our vessel through the waterway the ship was anchored off in the approach to the exit. This meant the deck watch were standing idle until dawn the next day, creating a golden opportunity to have a few beers and get paid for it. Big mistake! Halfway through my eight to twelve watch, my mate was called up to the bridge and told that the pilot was on his way out to our ship and that we would be sailing through the canal that night. We weighed anchor and began to manoeuvre towards the first lock. My watch mate and myself had to take the wheel at hourly intervals. Still feeling woozy from the copious amount of beer, I approached the wheelhouse in pitch darkness, and all I could see were illuminated dials and compass lights. I was trying to locate the storm step at the entrance of the wheelhouse and I tripped and fell flat on my face. I was ordered to leave the bridge and go down below, so my watch mate had to do two hours on the wheel. I lay on my bed and must have quickly dozed off.

The next morning, I was inevitably summoned to the old man's cabin. He didn't say a word, but I knew what was coming. He lectured me about drinking whilst on duty and that I was a 'disgrace to the company'. That was it. I knew from that moment with his fierce reputation that my card was well and truly marked for the duration of the voyage. He logged me four days' pay. During the passage over to New Zealand, most of us kept a low profile and worked as much overtime as we could to accumulate some funds for when we hit the Kiwi coast. I can't recall which port in New Zealand we called at first, but we eventually reached Littleton on the north end of the South Island. The local watering hole was aptly named The British. I was able to have a big sub from my earnings now that I had repaid the four days' deducted pay. So as soon as the gangway was down, the ship safely alongside, all deck work done, ie the derricks were topped (up) and all other duties duly completed, my mate Joe and I went ashore and headed for the renowned British.

The British Hotel where I hooked up with the landlady when I missed the ship

After spending almost five weeks at sea, it was time to let rip and have a good time. The next morning, I blearily awoke, still fully booted and spurred. I don't remember leaving the bar or even walking (or staggering) back to the ship. I couldn't recall a thing. Then came an almighty bang on my cabin door. It was the bosun shouting,

'Get your sorry arse out on deck, the first mate is on the warpath. Hardly anybody has appeared for work this morning!' My head was banging and I felt sick. I managed to stumble up to the messroom but couldn't face any food. I remembered an old trick to settle my stomach and asked the cook for an egg, cracked the shell and poured the slimy glutinous contents into a cup. I then added some cold milk, gave the sickly concoction a good stir and then (without hesitation!) tried to drink the slime. As I tilted the cup further towards my mouth, it just slid down my throat. I could feel it sticking as it descended down my stomach. How I kept it down I will never know, but within a minute, my stomach was lined, and I began to recover. We all say 'never again' when we feel sorry for ourselves, but the next night, sure enough - we went back to The British.

The landlady was very friendly towards me. She said that I had consumed a 'substantial' amount of beer, and many shots of navy dark rum. She had helped me to the exit, and put me and my mate into a taxi. I had taken a shine to her. She was rather a big girl, but with a nice and friendly personality. The ship was almost loaded and we were going to leave the next morning for the North Island. Me and-my mate Joe decided to pool the last of our money to have a last session in *The British* before we left. Another big mistake! Like Australian bars, Kiwi pubs served cold beer in jugs, so we ended up drinking many jugs rather than glasses of beer. By around nine that evening, the landlady and I were really becoming friendly with each other. It got to the point where we were becoming very close friends. I'm not sure what happened to my mate, I think he copped off with a girl as well. It was now nearly closing time and most of the customers were leaving. By around midnight, there was just my friendly lady and I. I ended up staying the night with her. The next morning, I located Joe who was in one of the upstairs rooms. I didn't ask what he had been up to as it wasn't hard to figure it out! We eventually bade our goodbyes and jumped into a taxi back to the ship. As we approached the berth where our ship was, we were horrified to see an empty space between two other ships - ours had left! That was it. We were totally on our own without much money left. All I could think of was our skipper's face when he had logged me the last time. Now we were in for it good and proper. We made our way back to the pub and as I approached the bar my lady friend looked at us in disbelief,

'Don't tell me, your ship has left!' she exclaimed.

'Yes,' I muttered.

'What are you both going to do now?' she asked, looking concerned.

'Haven't got a clue,' I replied despondently.

By this time, our funds were almost drying up. We had to try and contact the shipping agent in the hope that he would be able to reunite us with our vessel. Luckily for us, my new lady friend invited us both to stay at the pub until we could contact the agent and make our way back up north to our ship. Unfortunately for us, however, it was a bank holiday weekend and the agent was not available until the following Tuesday. Due to the warm friendship and welcome that our hostess had provided, we were able to stay until the agent had made all the necessary arrangements for us both to fly up to meet the ship in Napier. It was six days before we were both back on board, but needless to say, there was no welcoming committee. We were promptly ordered up to the captain's cabin, only this time he had the chief mate with him. I knew my days were numbered and that he would come down on me like the proverbial ton of bricks. After he had read the riot act to us both, a smirk stole over his red, blotchy face. Joe and I just looked at each other: now the moment had arrived for the punishment. It felt as though the jury in a court had just delivered their verdicts. The sentence was read out. He logged us both of eighteen days' pay (he had tripled up on the six days we were absent!) along with all the travel and flight expenses. He seemed to take a perverse pleasure in dishing out this penance upon us.

I was badly in debt to the shipping company and it would be a long time before I was back in the black, if ever. Now the writing was on the proverbial wall. In desperation, I started thinking about jumping ship (leaving the ship for good). The following morning, we were both expected to return to our duties, but my heart wasn't in it. I felt as though I was working for nothing (which I was). Our last port of call before we left Kiwi was Auckland. I knew that if I stayed on this ship with this particular skipper, I would be done for on our return to the UK. I was probably looking at a double DR: (declined to report, which was very bad) stamped in my discharge book. This was the worst action that could be taken. It meant that I would be lucky ever to return to sea again.

I made my mind up. I had to jump ship on the last night before the ship left for home. My mate Joe decided to stay and see the trip out because he wasn't in as much trouble as me. I spread the word to people that I could trust that I was leaving on our last night when it got dark. I had made some good friends on board, and they agreed with me that I had no choice but to jump ship. They had a whip-round for me and helped me to get my bags ashore without being noticed. I was very nervous and aware that if any of the officers got wind of my plan, or even worse, if they caught me making my way down the gangway with my gear in tow, my return journey would not be a pleasant one. I had met another girl while spending my last few days in Auckland; her name was also Diane. She helped me with the plan to travel out and away from Auckland as quickly as possible.

I waited for darkness to fall, but one of my biggest fears was if I were to be discovered missing, the officers would notify the ship's agent. That, in turn, would set off alarm bells, and the police would be alerted. If the police got involved, they could inform the airport authorities and the railway police. So, Diane suggested that we hitchhike all the way down to Wellington. Once we were clear of the docks, we headed for the main highway south. We had walked along gravel tracks at the side of the road, which we thought would provide us with some cover in case a cop car passed by. I was terrified of being picked up and sent back to Auckland before the ship had left. My mind and my thoughts were running riot. I even fretted that if we were picked up, Diane might turn me in to save her own skin. These things start to prey on your mind when you are in a strange country without much food or money. At one point, I phoned my brother Arthur from a callbox to give him the bad news. He warned me not to go into any bars when I arrived in Wellington, because the police were always patrolling the pubs on the lookout for underage drinkers, and at 19, I was well under the legal age. Eventually, we arrived in Wellington. We were both very hungry and needed a shower and to change our clothes. We entered a well-known seamen's watering hole The Bistro Bar inside the Royal Oak Pub.

We scoured the bar area to see whether Diane could recognise any of the girls that she used to hang out with. Just then, somebody from the other end of the bar shouted out to Diane. It was one of her friends who used to visit the British ships in Wellington Harbour. We felt relieved that we could talk and share a few beers with somebody trustworthy before we could call my brother to find us somewhere cheap for the night. I was very nervous, recalling my brother's warning. I went into the toilet, and when I emerged I noticed uniformed police patrolling the bar area. I trembled and shook uncontrollably; sweat trickled down my forehead and my armpits. I scanned the room for Diane, feeling abandoned and alone. We needed to get out of there fast. My imagination was running wild. *What if they were looking for me? Is this what it has come down to?* Worse still, had the skipper of my ship sent a search party for me? But then I thought, he couldn't have done, as he wouldn't know where I had gone after I jumped ship! I stood out like an escaped fugitive. I still had not set eyes on Diane, and this led to other terrible thoughts running riot in my already confused and over-stretched imagination. What if she had turned me into the police to protect her own skin? After all, I barely knew her. As I tried to manoeuvre my way across the gloomy room towards the front entrance, I was tapped on my shoulder, and someone growled. 'How old are you, sonny?' By now my jaw was rattling like the death rattle of a dying man. I didn't answer - I just froze.

'I just asked you your age, and you haven't answered me!' he barked.

I knew that I had to say something, just anything, in the hope that he would believe me and just let me go. But when his big hand had once more landed on my shoulder, I knew that this was it. I had blown any chance of getting out of there and escaping.

My life was about to be turned upside down. The police officer ordered me to hold out my hands while he handcuffed me, but I couldn't keep my hands still. My body language said it all: sweating, shaking and terrified. Diane then appeared and tried to talk him out of arresting me, but he wasn't having any of it. The officer questioned Diane and asked for some ID. After checking her driving license, he handed it back and told her she was in the clear and she could leave. But not me! He beckoned me to go outside towards his police car parked on the other side of the road. I guess he put it there so he could wander from bar to bar without drawing too much attention to himself. He opened the rear door, told me to sit in the back and then slammed the door (that had no interior door handles) shut. As he pulled away, the lights from the bar rapidly vanished and receded into the distance. I sat in the back facing forward, and there was a metal grille separating me from the front, making me feel like a captured and wanted criminal who had been at large and was now in custody awaiting his fate.

After what felt like an eternity, he pulled up to some big metal steel gates then leaned out towards the intercom. The gates squeaked as they slowly extended. He parked up next to a side door and beckoned me to get out of the car. How could I let this happen to me so soon after leaving Auckland? I asked him whether I could make a phone call to my brother. He suddenly looked alert and narrowed his eyes. His sudden reaction scared the hell out of me.

'So, you just arrived in this country with your brother?'

'No,' I shouted.

'I'm here with my girlfriend, just us two.'

'Oh, you have a brother here, so where does he live?'

I never answered him I just froze.

'I just asked you a *question*!' he snapped. 'Have you got a brother here in Wellington?'

'I'm not sure where he lives, I have his phone number.'

'How old is he then, is he younger or older than you?'

At this point I could hardly speak, I just muttered, 'Yeah, he's older than me.'

He fiddled with the handcuff keys, 'Okay, give me the number and I will find out for myself where he lives, then we will be paying him a visit.'

At this point I didn't want to drag my brother into this mess. But I had no choice, as I had already informed him about having a brother here in Wellington.

'I'm going to remove the cuffs so that you can give me his number.'

I put my sweating hand into my back pocket and extracted a piece of paper, with my brother's phone number scribbled across it in biro.

'I'll take that!' he snarled. He snatched it from me which made me more terrified of what was to come. Leaving the cuffs off for now, he led me into an interview room, then disappeared after locking the door behind him. He soon returned to tell me that he had called my brother to inform him of my arrest and to suggest he make his way down to the station. Despite it being my decision to jump ship, it had now turned into a living nightmare. I had to ask myself whether it had been worth it.

It was now about 10pm; I was hungry, tired, filthy and so fed up. Then the cell door opened and in walked my brother Arthur. The look on his face said it all.

'What the f...k have you done, you idiot? I warned you not to go in any bars. Now the shit has hit the fan, I don't know what will happen to you. But there's nothing I can do until morning, then I will come back here to see what they intend to do with you.' He looked sadly at me and shook his head slowly. 'Alan you have really made a balls-up of this, I'll have a word with the desk sergeant on the way out, but until then try to get some sleep in here. I'll be back first thing in the morning ... Bye.'

I knew he would have a go at me, but there was nothing I could do. I was where I was, and would just have to try and deal with it, only hoping to Christ my mother didn't get to hear about it. I didn't sleep too well on the cell bed, waking up several times in the night shivering and itching. Hell knows how many prisoners had slept on this mattress before me. The blanket that was provided smelt like it had just been scooped up out of the sewer. Even worse, the lightbulb that hung by a thread from the damp ceiling was left to glow all night. I think this was meant to be the beginning of my interrogation, and more was to follow to worsen my already bleak state of mind. I was hungry, thirsty and bloody cold. The en-suite luxury five-star toilet was a filthy stained, cracked basin that leaked its contents on to the thick, grimy and broken floor tiles.

When my brother arrived the next morning, he had a word with the desk sergeant, who told him that I would be shortly going to court and charged with illegal entry into New Zealand. The sergeant advised Arthur to hire a solicitor to advise me.

The next morning, I was informed that my brother had contacted a barrister, and had arranged to have me released on police bail conditional on my staying with Arthur until my court case. Then the same cop who had arrested me, gruffly told me that I would soon be leaving the police station and moved to a prison in Wellington. My heart just stopped.

'No officer! There must be some mistake - my brother has been told that I will be allowed out on bail!'

'I'm not sure about that, but in the meantime, you are to be shipped up the hill to the nick, where you will remain in custody until bail is confirmed.'

He chuckled mirthlessly, 'Hey, you will love it there with all the rest of the scum, murderers, thieves and paedophiles!'

How could they send me to prison when I had only jumped ship and been charged with underage drinking? This was a nightmare; they couldn't treat me like a hardened criminal. There were other prisoners in the adjoining cells and I could hear them shouting abuse at the police. Then a man shouted from his cell over in my direction.

'Hey, Pommy bastard - you ain't ever going home! Once you get put into Mount Crawford, you will be forgotten about.' He chuckled, 'The cons will love you up there, they will fight over you to become their bitch.'

As my tired eyes scanned the grubby, white walls of my cell, I noted all sorts of scribbled drawings etched onto the peeling paintwork and broken bricks. One that stood out read *all Pommys are bastards*. Another comment was *Maoris are s...t*.

None of this augured well for Mount Crawford; I didn't stand a chance of surviving there for long. Then the door opened from the police reception. In walked a cop with a bunch of keys dangling. He wore a smug grin on his unshaven face and inserted a big key into the lock and opened the door, which creaked ajar. He told me to follow him outside. My legs were shaking, and beads of sweat cascaded down. As we walked, I noticed the big white prison van at the entrance.

The driver and guard opened the two rear doors and ordered me in. There wasn't much light inside due to the blacked-out windows, but I could dimly see that it was fitted out like a cage to incarcerate animals with some seats on both sides. The guard barked,

'Sit your arse on one of them and don't move!'

After I sat down on the steel bench, the back doors slammed and the vehicle began to move forward. I was alone in there, off helpless to my fate. The light source was the dim lightbulb that swung to and fro as the vehicle rocked on its way.

I couldn't think straight and just felt blind panic and growing regret at my own stupidity. I could feel the truck slowing down and stopping with a jerk. The doors swung open, and as I looked out of the back I could see a courtyard with prisoners in uniform parading around the yard. Then a harsh voice screamed,

'Out you come, laddie! Come on; get your sorry ass out of here!'

He frogmarched me towards some double wooden doors then rattled the outsized knocker. Even the sound of the knocker seemed designed to instil fear. The doors opened to reveal the prison yard surrounded by the outer perimeter barbed wire. My knees were knocking; beads of perspiration ran down. The screws beckoned me to come inside.

'Come on, sonny, welcome to your new home. It could be a long time before you see the outside world again!'

As I strolled behind the officer, there were shouts and screams from the inmates as I got nearer to them.

'Hey, who do we have here?' shouted one of the inmates, 'you're a pretty little boy, aren't you?'

'What you in for, bitch?' screamed another prisoner. I didn't reply.

'Hey, honey, you could be my cellmate. I will take care of you.' The taunts never seemed to end. 'I would like you to be my 'bitch' you've got a pretty face, those hot lips of yours will come in handy...

As I was marched into the prison, the guard ordered me to empty the contents of my pockets onto the table and sign the form on a clipboard. Then I followed him into another room and he told me to strip down to my underwear and put on my prison uniform, which was the most embarrassing moment of my life. I was now officially a 'con'. I felt so alone and in despair. My life had gone from bad to worse in just a short time. How would my mother cope with this news if my brother wrote to her? When I had changed into my new 'Saville-Row' suit, I was ordered to stand against the back wall whilst holding a board with a set of numbers in white, across my chest. This was my mugshot and prison ID number. The only other time in my life that I had done this pose for a mugshot was when I had entered the Merchant Navy Training School, but that was for a good reason. Back then, I was full of hope and excitement, not black despair. I was exhausted and hungry. But instead of getting a hot meal, I was led to a cell just down the corridor. The screw opened the black cell door with a key from the bunch hanging from his belt.

'In, you go, sonny, it will soon be time to slop out and meet your new roommate,' he said, not without sympathy.

I didn't know whether he was joking or not, but somehow, I knew he wasn't. He told me to get into the cell and closed the door behind him. I introduced myself to my (hopefully) short-term cellmate. He was a six-foot Maori, with a scar across the right side of his face. His teeth were as black as his skin. I hesitated before I looked him in the eye, then I said with a quivering lower lip,

'My ... my ... my name is Alan - what's yours?'

He never answered, just growled and sat on the lower bunk, which left me in no doubt who would be sleeping on the top. The stench in the cell was overpowering and there was not enough room to swing a cat. In the far corner, there was a filthy bucket - our 'en-suite bathroom'. The cell window was about one foot by one foot and sited three-quarters of the way up the back wall, with six rusty steel bars running end to end. I was now famished and exhausted after all that I had been through on my first day of incarceration. I didn't dare ask my new companion what time dinner would be served. I thought that I would just climb on my poky bunk and try to sleep. I attempted to haul myself up by standing on the lower bunk but felt a big pull on my ankle.

'Get yeer fuckin foot off my bunk, yeh Pommy bastard.'

By this time, I was drained and I got to the stage where I didn't care less if I got my head kicked in - I just wanted to sleep. I was expecting this thug to haul me from my bunk and give me a battering, but he left me alone, probably saving it for another time when he would take his anger out on me. As I tried to sleep, the day's events just kept churning around in my head like a washing machine on a fast spin. The stench from my pillow and the half-torn blanket was enough to make anyone throw up, but I don't think that I had anything left in my gut to bring to the surface of my aching stomach. Just as I was drifting off to sleep, there was an almighty scream from another cell just somewhere close to mine. I jumped up without thinking and banged my head on one of the rusty, old pipes that ran along the ceiling.

'Forrr fuck sake, Pommy, what are you fucking dooin?' growled the Kiwi.

Mount Crawford Prison Wellington New Zealand 'Wellington Library, 2020.'

Happily, it wasn't too long before I was released on bail, which came with some strict conditions. An order was put in place that I had to stay with my brother and nowhere else. I had to report to the Wellington harbour police at least once a week until my deportation back to the UK. The other primary condition was that I had to find a temporary job to support myself and not sponge off the state. It wasn't too long before I found employment with a local painting and decorating company. I was sincere and straight with them about my situation because sooner or later, I would have to leave.

Months had passed by without any contact from the shipping agents or any other authorities who would notify me when a British merchant ship would be sailing from the New Zealand coast to deport me back to the UK. The main reason for this is that my bail stipulated that it had to be a vessel sailing to the UK without calling at any other countries or ports, in case I jumped ship again. This worked in my favour as I was having the time of my life: no worries, a roof over my head with food to eat and living in an apartment with my brother and his pals.

As time went by, rumours were going around at the company where I worked. Cutbacks were being made and this worried me because the conditions of my bail were that I had to have a job so that I wouldn't be claiming any benefits. I recall having a chat with the supervisor about my fears of being laid off. He assured me that I would be safely working for them until it was time for me to go home, which was a great relief. It had paid off being honest and upfront about my predicament. The authorities eventually informed me that there was a ship in Auckland that would be sailing to London in the next couple of days. Arrangements would be made for me to travel there by train from Wellington to Auckland, and my travel documents would arrive soon.

So, this was it. The dreaded time had arrived. I was despondent as I had harboured dreams of living in this country for a long time to come. I picked up mail from the doormat one morning, as usual searching for something official-looking with my name on it. My envelope stood out from the rest: a large brown package with a New Zealand Government stamp on the top right-hand corner. I hesitated. My hands were sweaty and shaking; this could be what I was expecting, yet dreading. I didn't open it straight away but just stood and stared at it lying on the table. I just peeled the sticky folded end of the envelope back and peered at the name on the top of one of many sheets. Yes, this was it, the dreaded time had arrived. Along with my detailed instructions was a one-way rail ticket from Wellington to Auckland. But what did surprise me was how long the journey time was. The train would be leaving around lunchtime but not arriving in Auckland until early the next morning. I knew that it would be a long and lonely journey, but I didn't expect to travel overnight. My comfortable world had collapsed. The show was over, no more good times, only the unknown lay ahead.

I sat alone in the empty flat with my head in my hands thinking to myself whether there was any way out. My mind was running wild, even my wildest ideas had to be jettisoned as I had no money and no contacts other than this place. No, I just had to face up to what was on the cards for me.

Around 5pm that evening, everybody returned home after their day's work. My brother asked me why I looked so sad but before I could even speak he said,

'Have you had some bad news?'

'Yes,' I murmured.

'Go on then tell me what it is, but I think I can guess. You've had a letter telling you that it's time to go home, I can read you like a book.'

'Yes, I have. There's a ship in Auckland and it's sailing to London in three days. I've got to travel by train and board the ship tomorrow.

'Wow, that's quick!' my brother exclaimed.

'Yes, it is! There's a train pass in the envelope which I have to exchange for a ticket at the station. I'll have to contact my employers to let them know the situation. I'd better start packing.'

We knew that it was going to happen, but it still came as a shock. I wished I could have stayed for good. Who knew what was waiting for me back home where I would have to report to the shipping federation in Salford.

That night we had a little leaving party. It helped me relax and reflect on what I had done in my short time in New Zealand, along with many good friends that I would be leaving behind. I hoped to return someday and revisit my brother and his friends. The next morning (sporting a sore head), I then ordered a taxi to the station, said my goodbyes and that was it. The ticket office clerk at the station exchanged my documents for a one-way second-class trip to Auckland. Then as I turned to leave, the guy called me back and said,

'Don't you want your pillow and blanket? It's a long journey and there are no sleeper cabins on this train. You have to get your head down on the seats!'

I couldn't believe that I would ever be walking through a train laden with–bedding; it made me feel like a real down-and-out. I bagged a window seat which was handy for leaning against to sleep and to view the scenery. I was the sole occupant as the train pulled away, leaving me melancholy and regretting bitterly what I was leaving behind. I fretted non-stop about what lay ahead and what sort of trip I would have on the long, five weeks sailing to London. The train journey was also a long one. I recall slipping in and out of an intermittent doze then waking with a disoriented jerk. Eventually, a distorted voice from the carriage's radio speaker crackled that we were nearing Auckland station. I gathered up all my worldly goods and disembarked, and headed to a waiting taxi. As I wasn't sure where the docks were, I had to show the driver my paperwork. It was only a short drive down to the harbour, which was just as well as money was in short supply. I had a couple of hundred dollars of emergency funds that my brother and friends had collected for me to get me through the difficult times that I would face upon my return and had also been issued with a note to hand to the authorities in London Docks. This authorised them to issue a train travel warrant to Manchester.

I paid off the cab then walked the short distance to my ship. I recall that it was one of the *Shaw-Savill's* vessels. Because I wasn't signing onto this ship as official crew, I would be deported as a DBS (Disabled British Seaman). This was common practice, even though I wasn't actually 'disabled'. It was a maritime ruling that meant that I would be entitled to full board on my voyage back to the UK. I reported to the chief officer and told him who I was, then checked-in with the chief steward who told me where my cabin was situated and he gave me a key to my 'home' for the next five weeks.

The layout of the accommodation was similar to the ship that I had left, so it was easy to find my way around. I shared a cabin with two other DBS seamen, so they were in the same boat as me – literally! After I had unpacked my gear, I made my way up top to the messroom. There were other crew members seated and eating their food. As I entered the room, I did say 'hi' to the guys facing me on the other table, but it was a one-way greeting. From that moment on, I didn't feel welcome or part of the ship's company. I wasn't the only one who had bad feelings about the atmosphere onboard the ship; my other two companions felt the same as me. As the day went by, there wasn't much to keep my mind occupied other than to read books and play cards with my temporary roommates. I knew that this voyage home was going to be a drag because we weren't allowed to do any work. Several times a week there were activities in the crew bar such as darts competitions and card games. As money was short, I knew that I couldn't spend too much money onboard because I didn't know what lay ahead at home for me so I just bought a couple of beers on those nights. There was an unwritten rule amongst British seamen to look after any sailor in distress or who were without any money. However, on this particular ship, a sense of brotherhood was out of the question. Everybody just seemed to be one big clique and outsiders weren't welcome. The days and weeks passed, and we finally arrived back in the Port of London. I was given my instructions and travel warrant back to Manchester.

The only money that I had to my name was about £25 remaining from the whip round that my flatmates had given me. I had to use this pittance to get me back home. I managed to get a free ride in a cab to Euston Station with one of the more considerate crew members. It was then a long, miserable journey to Manchester, not knowing what my fate was going to be when I reported to the shipping federation in Salford. I couldn't afford the cab fare home from Manchester Piccadilly Station, so I had to carry my gear to the bus station and catch the 101 to Wythenshawe. I felt as though I had died, left heaven and woken up in hell. My life had gone full circle, from poverty to a great career in the Merchant Navy then back to my broken family life.

Not only did I think that I would never return to sea again but I also had nowhere to live. Despite never venturing out, my mother had apparently met a bloke somewhere. It came as a great shock to Arthur and me. She had 'fled the nest' and moved to North Wales, supposedly living in a caravan with my brother Michael and my sisters. What kind of life did they have, living in a shoebox? I discovered that he was an unemployed heavy drinker. It baffled me that she had seen fit to take the kids to the middle of nowhere, with no money, and remove them from their friends and schools. This created a lot of problems. I needed a permanent address before I could report to the shipping federation. I managed to get the address of my eldest brother David and his wife Angela from his mother-in-law. They lived above a shop in a one-bedroomed flat and were sympathetic to my plight. They let me kip on the floor (beggars can't be choosers!).

His flat was tiny – you couldn't swing a cat in it. I had to walk into the bathroom sideways because the bath, toilet and sink occupied the best part of the room. The shower was nothing more than a flimsy pipe with one small nozzle hanging from the end. After trying to control the water temperature, I admitted defeat; it was either too hot or too cold. So, despite the lack of home comforts I took him up on his offer and after a lousy night's sleep, I showered and headed down to Salford Docks to see the federation superintendent. I fervently hoped that if they needed an AB to join a ship immediately, then my committee meeting could just be a formality.

By the time I gave my details at reception, my palms were sweating. I was shaking. Could this be the end of my short career at sea? I never thought that my dilemma could have led to this.

'He will see you now,' said the officer, 'second door on the left, knock before entering.'

The only thing that was knocking was my knees. As I tapped on the door, a deep voice sounded rumbled,

'Come and sit down next to my desk. When did you get back to the UK?'

'Two days ago, Sir.'

'This meeting is for you to give me your side of the story,' he explained, 'then I will inform you of the report that I received from the Captain of the *M.V. Majestic*. When the interview is concluded, I will decide on what action will be taken against you. Do you understand what I have just said?'

'Yes, I mean yes *Sir*, I do.'

His eyebrows moved upwards, although not wholly unkindly. 'Now tell me briefly why you missed the ship in Auckland, and if there were any circumstances that made you decide to leave the vessel before returning to the UK.'

I now had my chance to tell my side of the story so the words tumbled out. 'It all started after sailing from Odessa, on through the Panama Canal. We were at anchor waiting to transit the Canal. We were informed that we wouldn't be entering the Canal Zone until sometime the next morning so we were put on standby until the pilot boarded the ship. This meant that my watch mate and I could just keep an eye on the ship whilst at anchor. But there was a party going on in one of the steward's cabins. I called in on them to see if everything was okay and then had a beer shoved into my hand (common practice amongst the crew). One beer led to another, and another and before too long I had had more than I should have done whilst performing my watch-keeping duties. That was when my watch mate appeared at the cabin door and informed me that we would be transiting the Canal shortly.'

The superintendent nodded occasionally and scribbled on his paper. I could not read it as it was upside down and his expression remained sphinx-like throughout.

'Go on,' he said, 'what next?'

'I replied to my watch mate that we couldn't be transiting as we were meant to be at anchor until the morning. My watch mate told me that the pilot was on his way and arriving in about ten minutes. He asked me to get on deck and to help him to put the pilot ladder over the starboard side.'

The administrator gestured encouragingly and I felt a little more optimistic so ploughed on with my sorry tale.

'There was still three hours of my watch left. I would take my turn at the wheel although I was not in a fit state. But I was left with no choice so when I entered the wheelhouse in the dark, I tripped over the storm step at the entrance to the bridge. After picking myself up, I proceeded to navigate my way towards my watch mate to relieve him of the wheel. But before I could take over, the skipper came over to me and said, 'You've been drinking!' I didn't have a chance to challenge his accusation. He ordered my mate to stay at the helm, and he told me to leave the bridge. The next morning, I was summoned up to his cabin, and he laid into me with all kinds of threats. Then he informed me that he would log me three days' pay. From then on, I knew that he had marked my card, and he would have it in for me for the rest of the voyage.'

I waited for a response. The superintendent nodded but said nothing...

'We were in the port of Littleton South Island of Kiwi, and it was a bank holiday, so we did have a couple of days off. This is where I missed the ship after it sailed to other ports on the North Island. It was about six days before I re-joined the ship. Once again, I was hauled up in front of the captain who logged me eighteen days' pay. He multiplied by three on the six days it took me to return. He left me in no doubt that I wasn't welcome on his ship. I told him about my fear of being on a ship where my card was effectively marked. Being young and impulsive I had made the decision to jump ship without thinking it through.'

The superintendent shuffled his notes and coughed. Looking stern, he summed up and delivered his verdict.

'Okay. I have read the log from the skipper and in his view, you were not capable of performing your duties. You took it upon yourself to leave the ship in Auckland. After taking into consideration your excellent record up until this incident, I have decided to give you a second chance, but if you come before me again at any time, your career at sea will be over. Have I made myself clear, young man?'

My throat was parched, but I managed to say, 'Yes, Sir, I understand, and I won't let you down.'

'That will be all, and you may leave now.'

'Thank you, Sir.'

After all the worrying, it was all over, and I could go back to sea. I felt like celebrating, but I didn't have much money left so I went back to David's place and told him the good news. He was pleased for me, so I thought while he was in a good mood I would tap him up for a small loan to see me through until I got my first ship - he loaned me fifty quid. I gave my brother's contact details to the shipping federation (no mobiles then), so if they needed to get hold of me for a job, I didn't want to let them down or miss out on a ship.

It was lucky for me that it was near Christmas and New Year when no married sailor wanted to leave his family. It wasn't too long before I received a telephone call from the Poole (shipping federation) informing me that there was a vacancy for an AB on the *Manchester Crusade*, sailing from Salford on the 30th of December. The man asked me whether I wanted to take this job and I didn't hesitate. *Yes, Yes, Yes, please!* It was my only opportunity to get a clear stamp in my discharge book. Once I had completed this voyage, I would have a clean slate, and my last bad discharge would be history.

To keep on the right side of the shipping federation, I decided to stay with *Manchester Liners* for the meantime and signed a contract with the company to secure my future employment. After about a year with *Liners*, I met the woman who was to become my future wife, her name was Deirdre. Before we knew it, she became pregnant with our first child Rachel, and I decided that I needed to be home to help with childcare. I consequently got a job shore-side with a frozen food company working mostly night shifts. I found it very difficult to adapt to home life; I was always unhappy and miserable, with the repetitive monotonous job. Inevitably, I started to take some nights off work but this didn't go down too well with the management. Then my wife told me that she was pregnant with our second child; this narrowed my options even more.

Right page: my discharge book. shows VNC (voyage not complete)

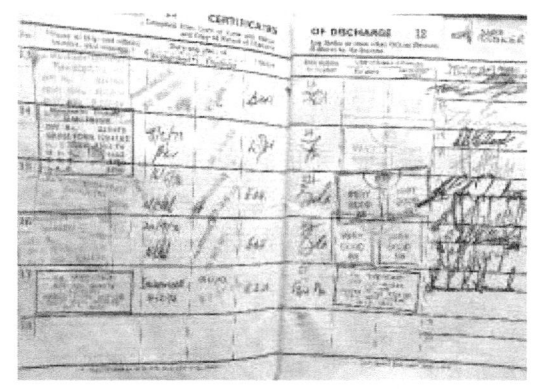

*Right page shows a double stamp VERY GOOD VERY GOOD.
I was now able to continue my career at sea.*

This depressing lifestyle went on for about four years; the same routine day-in, day-out. Being unable to go to sea did not suit me at all; it made me feel useless and miserable. I began to put on weight, because I was always eating in the day and on the night shifts. I knew that something had to change. My daughter, Rachel, was now about four years old and our new-born boy, Paul, arrived in March 1977. I felt so depressed and longed for the happy days when I was at sea. I felt as though life was slipping away from me. I really missed the life at sea, the camaraderie, seeing different countries and cultures, the way of life, and the freedom of the sea, it was such a great way to get paid for seeing how the other half lives.

I decided to re-apply to go back to sea, but wasn't very optimistic about the application and interview. To my great surprise, and good fortune I was accepted, subject to passing the medical (which I did). It wasn't too long after my acceptance that I received a phone call from the federation informing me that there was a job going on the *Manchester Concorde*, and would I be willing to sail on her the next day (how could I refuse?). I didn't sleep much that night, tossing and turning. Was this a golden opportunity to rekindle my life and to start living again, no more a hermit? You never leave the sea, and it never leaves you.

The next morning, I dusted the four years' worth of cobwebs from my old suitcase in the attic and packed my work clothes, jeans, socks and oilskins, along with my sea boots (wellingtons). The atmosphere in the house was tense and silent as the time neared to leave my kids and my wife behind. I knew from her body language that she didn't want me to leave. I decided that I needed to clear the air and confide in her how unhappy I was, and I needed to return to the job and life I once had. She didn't respond, just nodded her head whilst drawing on a cigarette.

The only sound to break the fraught silence was that of my daughter's wooden building blocks tumbling on the floor as she played, oblivious to the tension between her parents. Heaven forbid if she decided to throw one at me for leaving. Now I started to feel selfish and guilty for leaving my family behind. Despite my guilt, I had to go through with this one and only opportunity to get my life back from the brink of disaster. I could have stayed at sea like many other fathers who just left their wives to get on with it, but I had given up my freedom, independence and above all my happiness to do what I thought was the right thing and it had backfired spectacularly.

The half-hour wait for the cab felt like a lifetime. Each time I looked at my watch, my wife would snap that I couldn't wait to leave them behind, piling the guilt on my already fragile wellbeing. The taxi arrived and I didn't want to make a fuss, so I just picked up my bags and made my way towards the front door, with my wife and Rachel in tow. It was difficult for me to leave like this, but I knew it would work out so I wasted no time climbing into the cab. The driver asked me where I was going and I just replied, 'Salford Docks please'. As he pulled away, I felt a wave of guilt and emotion then as I turned around I saw the silhouettes of two figures moving behind the net curtains. That was the last sight of my family for some time to come. But deep down I knew that I had made the right decision, and the emotional scars of me leaving them for the first time, would soon heal.

Twenty minutes later, I arrived at the shipping federation. The building–had not changed at all in over four years with its creaking front door and flaking brownie-green paint. The same assistant supervisor was there, always a pleasant chap, with a moustache that curled at the ends and old-school, retro, brown-rimmed specs. He asked me for my ragged discharge book and union card and noted that it had been over four years since I last went to sea. He looked for my application to confirm my acceptance back into the federation's system.

'Okay,' he replied, 'everything's in order; follow me into the back room where the doctor will examine you before we give you the all-clear. Then go to nine dock where the *Manchester Concorde* is berthed.' He paused, then pondered, 'Bet you find it strange coming down here again after working shore-side for so long?'

'Yes, I do, Sir, very strange indeed.' The examining doctor was a scrawny little man with a ragged collar around which was draped a stethoscope. As he peered over his dropped spectacles, he said in a gravelly voice,

'Here boy, let me give you the once over.'

After the mini-medical and blood pressure check, he signed a slip of paper, and mumbled to me to take it back to the man at the front desk so that he could stamp my book. That's all there was to it. I was now officially back on my way to returning to my old self and a new way of life.

I had already sailed on this ship, so I knew what she was like. I looked up at her red and white hull with its thick rust marks around the anchor where the claws of the giant steel hulk had torn its way through the metal to reveal its inner core. Mooring ropes sagged as the ship was taking on loaded containers. Debris was floating in between the ship's side and the dock, everything from old, broken, wooden pallets and a variety of plastic bottles, to empty beers cans and dead, smelly fish. All this stained the bottom of the hull, so that when a tugboat disrupted the water, it left scummy tidemarks like a bathtub that had been emptied and not cleaned out.

I climbed aboard and made my way to the messroom so that I could leave my bag somewhere and locate the chief steward's cabin to collect my cabin key. On entering the mess, a few seamen of diverse nationalities were having their 'smoko' (tea break). 'Hi,' I hailed to a wall of ominous silence. This immediate unfriendliness wasn't what I expected. After dumping my bag, I located the steward and collected a bunch of unlabelled keys which I had to sift through in various locks. Eventually I found an empty berth. After this, all that was left to do was report to the second mate and sign on. That was it, I was officially back at sea where I belonged.

The bosun informed us all that the vessel would be sailing the next day, so in the messroom 'smoko' I introduced myself to the lads who, unlike when I first said hello, the crew seemed a lot friendlier. The system for working out who went on which of the three watches would be determined by cutting a pack of cards, between the six ABs comprising two men in a watch. The high card went for the most popular shift, the four to eight; then the eight to twelve and the 'graveyard watch' of twelve to four. These shifts were for the duration of four hours, twice a day. If there was any overtime available, then that would be worked in between these shift patterns. Luck was on my side. I pulled out an Ace - the four to eight was mine along with another lucky man, Joe. We were crewmates for the whole trip. The next morning, we left at nine dock and navigated the Manchester Ship canal. This voyage would take us across the North Atlantic to Montreal, then on through the Great Lakes to several Canadian and North American ports with which I was already familiar from my previous *Manchester Liners* ships. Once we had cleared the Irish coast and dropped the pilot, it was about a five-day crossing to Canada. Much of the work was familiar stuff but it was a joy to experience the clean, pure air whilst on lookout on the wing of the bridge. I felt alive again not only mentally but also physically.

I had many regrets about leaving my family behind but I knew in my heart that I had made the right decision. I was now back in the swing of things after making several more trips with *Manchester Liners* and there was no going back to that miserable lifestyle as a civilian. Each trip away became more routine and less stressful for my wife and children and allowed them to become accustomed to their altered way of life. It was like a new lease of life, out with the old and in with the new.

One day, whilst at sea, I received a letter from my wife informing me that our daughter Rachel, had had an accident whilst riding on her bike. She had fallen off and one end of the steel handlebars had penetrated her cheek. I felt terribly guilty for not being there when I was needed. I phoned home once we were in port. The news wasn't encouraging; Rachel had to have stitches on her cheek. My wife was upset, but she seemed to be coping. On my return home, I took one look at her pretty little face and could have cried. She was such a lovely young girl but her injury was worse than I expected; she had a scar about one and a half inches long. I was devastated as this mark could be with her for life. I wasn't happy with how the stitching had been carried out; it looked more like a rush job by the local butcher than that of a surgeon. Her face was swollen with deep brown skin tissue on the surface of her cheekbone. My world had just fallen apart, how could I go back to sea and leave them like this? My little girl for whom I had given up my own happiness to stay ashore and work in a miserable factory.

After a few days I received a call to report back to the *Manchester Liners* office. I had to report for duty on the *Manchester Concord*. It broke my heart to leave both my wife and Rachel to deal with the aftermath of the accident. I worried about how she would cope with all the emotional trauma that she would have to face at school and with her friends.

It was the 8th of December 1980. Whilst on lookout I heard an announcement over the radio in the wheelhouse. The sounds were distorted and breaking up, but I could just make out the news that John Lennon had been shot. I beckoned to the third mate who was on watch in the wheelhouse. I asked him whether he had heard the sad news.

'Yes,' he replied. John Lennon was dead, but he wasn't sure how he had been killed. It wasn't until we reached our first port that the report was confirmed, he had been gunned down by a deranged fan at the Dakota building where he lived in New York.

Then in early 1981, I decided to make a move from *Manchester Liners*. After reporting to the shipping federation in Liverpool, I was offered the *M.V. Oroya*, berthed at Birkenhead and owned by the Pacific Steam Navigation company. This voyage would take us through the Panama Canal then onto the west coast of South America. It was a move away from the mundane routine of crossing the North Atlantic which was an unforgiving journey when made in the harsh Canadian winter weathers of treacherous seas and hazardous icebergs. The voyage lasted about three months. After leaving the west coast, we sailed through the Caribbean and called at

Jamaica to discharge some of the cargo from Peru. This was an enjoyable experience as I hadn't ventured this far down the Southern Ocean before and the voyage allowed me to broaden my horizons and discover cultures that were different from those of North America. After leaving the Caribbean, we headed back to the UK and signed off in Avonmouth.

After spending some much-needed leave with my family, I joined what was (although I had no idea at the time) my last posting as a merchant seaman. The bulk-carrier, *M.V. Lynton Grange* was part of the Holder Marine Company. I flew out to Rotterdam and had been led to believe that the trip would be about four months' duration. However, we soon learned that there were no orders for this ship, so no one knew where we would be sailing to. It was what is known as a 'Tramp ship', meaning a vessel with only a limited number of orders from its shipping company because it was on charter. The uncertainty was a hammer blow to me and to my family; had I known this at the time of signing on, I wouldn't have taken this job. We never knew from one day to another where we were going, and this wasn't good for on board morale. Considering that an ABs salary was very low, confidence amongst the crew was at rock bottom, to say the least. We were paid monthly while still signed on to the ship's articles *(terms and conditions)*. That was the only good news because many of the crew had families back home who relied on the monthly payments from their partners. After a few weeks had passed, the ship's master was given orders to sail for the USA to load cargos for Europe. This improved morale amongst the crew and they began to readjust to a more productive life at sea.

I can't stress enough how unpredictable and dangerous this job could be. It was while we were at anchor in Baltimore, that the first mate decided he wanted the ship's bow painted which involved rigging stages. (These were long planks of wood with a cross piece at each end (like horns) with ropes hanging from the top of the rails secured around both ends of the horns with hitch that we used to lower the stage down when necessary.

This image shows what the stage looked like. One guy sits at one end, and the other sits on the other both are able to lower the stage while they are both seated on it.

To get back to the top we used a rope ladder, known as a Jacob's ladder (just like a trapeze artist would use at a circus show) over the side of the bow. Because this ship had a massive flare on the bow (the curved shape) it meant that the stages, when rigged and hanging over the sharp end, would just hang down in thin air like a swinging circus trapeze. The flare on the bow had small rings welded at various points so that a rope with a hook on one end could be lassoed onto the ringbolts. Once the hooks were latched onto the rings, the sailors would haul themselves towards the flare on the bow, a practice known as 'bowsing-in'. It was a crude way of hauling oneself in towards the great hulk of the sharp end. Once we made the wooden stages secure, it meant that the two sailors on each stage would be pulled into the 'sharp end' (the bow).

This was very unsafe and meant that the lads would be up against the sharp end at an angle. Once secure to the bow, it was challenging to try and stand up on the wooden stage plank and paint with a very long-handled, paint-laden roller whilst holding on to the ropes with one hand. The whole manoeuvre felt like a trapeze act dangling from a tightrope. Health and safety was non-existent at the time; so, there was no such thing as a harness. We just had to get on with it. I was a terrified non-swimmer; one false move and the guy at the other end of the stage and I would end up in the water. Inevitably, this did happen. One of the ABs working on a stage further along the bow fell into the drink. I didn't see him fall - I just heard the splash as he hit the water. The shouts went up to the man who was attending us from the fo'c'sle head. We all looked over the gunnel (rail) to see whether we could spot the man once we had got back onboard. He was nowhere to be seen and despite one sailor jumping off his stage and swimming around the bow to look for him, there was no sign. He had disappeared without trace below the icy cold water of Baltimore harbour. The skipper was informed, and he radioed the port authority police who sent out search teams and used dragnets to try and recover the man. After several hours they recovered his body which was then taken ashore to be repatriated to his family.

We were all devastated at losing someone whom we had sailed with and for him to go in that way. Morale was at an all-time low on this ship. I just wanted to get off. During the next few weeks, mainly while I was on lookout on the bridge on dark and lonely nights, I began to hallucinate. Each time that I looked around the corners of the bridge, I could see my shipmate who had vanished below the sea. Even after leaving the vessel while on leave, I could see his ghost-like silhouette staring at me. I felt as though I was suffering from survivor's guilt. I have never forgotten this tragic incident, and the nightmares will stay with me forever.

It was after we arrived at another port on the American Eastern Seaboard that tragedy struck again. I was night watchman and whilst patrolling the foredeck, I could hear shouts from the offshore side of the ship. I frantically ran along the foredeck, slipping on the frozen ice. I peered over the side and I could just make out the silhouette of somebody scrambling onto some broken ice. As I drew nearer, the cries became louder. He was begging for help and I now recognised him as the third officer. He seemed to be in great difficulty and flailing at me to get to him and rescue him from the dark, icy waters in the sea off Norfolk Virginia. But the memories of losing a friend in Baltimore not so long ago gave me the strength and courage to scrabble over to this poor soul (even though I couldn't swim). Oblivious to my own safety, I clambered down the frozen pilot ladder that was secured to the rails, then tied the safety line around my waist but this was proving to be a difficult task. The biting cold had stiffened my already frozen hands and I could barely move my rigid body towards his cries for help, whilst at the same time hanging on for dear life. I clambered over the broken chunks of ice on the surface of the water. I wasn't sure if they would be thick enough for me to crawl along as I made my way to the sounds of a desperate man I managed to grab hold of his arm and somehow tug on the safety rope.

My own strength was rapidly dissipating but somehow, after grabbing hold of his coat and scrambling over the ice, we made it towards the ladder where we were hauled up onto the deck. We both had some explaining to do to the skipper after we had thawed out. But to my surprise (and relief) the third officer did all the talking. To my amazement, the captain moved closer to where I was standing (shivering) and held out his huge hand. His gold braid bristled under the fluorescent light as he gave me a very firm handshake, and barked in his deep Scottish accent,

'Well done laddie, you've just saved a man's life... and this won't be forgotten. Now make your way down to the chief steward's cabin and tell him to give you a litre size bottle of *Four Bells* rum and for him to charge it to me. Take the rest of the day off and get pissed under my orders. See that you do, laddie. It's not every day that a skipper orders a rating to get hammered, but on this occasion, and only on this occasion, I was excused.

When a ship is launched, a bottle of Champagne is smashed onto the vessel's hull. Superstition has it that if it doesn't break on the first attempt, the ship is doomed for life. Could this have happened when the *M.V. Lynton Grange* left the builder's yard? It certainly seemed dogged by bad luck. Eventually I was paid off in Nagasaki in Japan and flew home back to my family. This was not how I wanted to end my career in the Merchant Navy.

CHAPTER FOUR

1982: THE OFFSHORE INDUSTRY - BIGGEST MISTAKE OF MY LIFE

I had only been on leave for two days when I received a 'phone call from head of personnel at Houlder Marine in London. He informed me that they had nominated me for the Royal Humane Society Award for rescuing and saving the life of an officer onboard a ship. There was going to a presentation ceremony held in my honour in Manchester.

The Manchester Evening News would be writing and publishing my story. This came as a big surprise to me. I felt like a celebrity. After receiving the award, it was time for my family and me to celebrate this once in a lifetime achievement.

Having lost one of my mates in Baltimore and coming to the rescue of another officer in the freezing waters of Virginia, I decided it was time I learnt to swim. I signed up for lessons at my local swimming baths in Sharston Wythenshawe. I knew that it wouldn't be easy because of my age, and because I was still having the occasional nightmare about that poor guy in Baltimore. I didn't ever want to be in that situation again where I couldn't help and then had to live with the survivor's guilt after the incident.

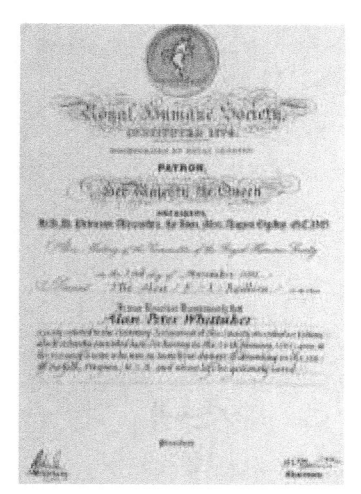

My award from The Royal Humane Society

After having a chat with the instructor, I decided on the breaststroke method because it didn't require me to have my face down in the water while swimming. The depth of the water began at the shallow end about three foot, then it went further down the deep end to twelve foot. This was more of an ordeal because I just couldn't synchronise my arms and legs while trying to breathe at the same time. Because I was so determined to succeed no matter how difficult it would be for me, I wasn't going to give up.

I decided to go to the swimming baths every single day, seven days a week until I achieved what I set out to accomplish. After several disappointing sessions in the cold and becoming accustomed to swallowing water and chlorine, which also reddened my eyes, I began to swim a few feet at a time. After many more gruelling sessions I felt confident to jump in at the deep end and tread water to the surface. (I wasn't sure if I would make it back to the surface.) I would never win any Olympic medals, but I could swim enough if I ever found myself in difficulty or a similar situation that I had found myself in before at sea.

As for returning to the deep sea, I was not sure if I would ever go back. There seemed to be news going around that many shipping companies were using cheap foreign labour, recruiting seamen and catering staff from overseas, such as from the Philippines and South America. Houlder Marine operated oilrigs in the North Sea. Many of their deep-sea personnel had moved over to the rigs along with catering crews.

It was around April 1982 that I decided I would take advantage of my celebrity status and my award and the perks that might come my way. I wrote to the head of HR about moving over to the oil division of the North Sea (it's not what you know, but who you know) and made further enquiries about working on one of their installations. A few days later, I received a phone call from HR offering me a position on the *Kingsnorth UK* drilling rig as an Able Seaman. I mulled this over for only a short while, then called the office back to accept the job. I was not sure whether I had made the right decision but was optimistic and excited about my future and what this new role would mean, particularly as it meant I could spend more time at home with my family. The tours of duty offshore were a fortnight on, a fortnight off, with four weeks annual leave. It was common knowledge that the oil industry paid high salaries to its workers. I could not miss this golden opportunity to change my career and to have the chance of earning good money.

I received my contract, travel arrangements and instructions, which were to travel to Aberdeen and make my way to the hotel near Dice Airport. A representative from the company met me at the hotel reception and informed me that they had booked me into the Skean-Dhu Dyce hotel also known locally as the 'Ski and Doo') hotel.

The following morning a minibus transported me and the other crewmembers who were going out to join this rig to the heliport. There were strict health and safety (but not offshore at this time) procedures at the airport. They were more stringent than flying from a commercial airport because of the oil industry's strict safety policy.

I had sailed with many Scots and Geordies whilst at sea. Still, some of this bunch were from the Outer Hebrides and other Scottish islands. Many were crofters from sheep farms and I could not understand a word they were saying. I bet they had never seen so many people in any one place at any one time! Once we were all suited and booted, we waited for the call to embark on the rigorous security procedure. They would bar anybody who had been drinking the night before and who was still intoxicated. A dismissal would invariably ensue.

There were several helicopters on the tarmac, some with their rota blades whirling around, and very noisy too. The attendant directed us to the nearest one facing the control tower and its rotor blades churned and generated a downdraft that caused the wind to blow in our direction. I clutched onto my holdall to avoid it disappearing into the engine's air intakes. This was not luxury travel. I was the third person to mount the steps that led into this steel capsule and as I walked down the narrow aisle, I had to lean forward so as not to bang my head on the overhead lockers. There was a space halfway down the short passage so I parked my backside on the cold leather seat. After donning a pair of ear protectors, I put my seatbelt on. A crackling radio announced that we would be taking off then flying out over the Shetland Islands. The journey would take about two hours so we should land on the rig before noon. There seemed to be no heating inside the chopper. I was freezing even though I had my survival suit on, which provided me with some warmth. The person next to me was having a nap and snoring, something I could not do due to the tremendous noise. We flew over what I was told was Peterhead Prison. The weather was predictably grim: heavy rain and not much to see outside the window. Many thoughts were swirling around in my head, as I had never flown over the North Sea in a helicopter – a dramatic entry into a new life.

I have always said, 'as one door closes another one opens. I hoped that this next 'open door' would open wide and lead to a happy life. The captain eventually came back over the radio to announce that that we were landing on the *Kingsnorth UK* rig.

I could already see the jumbo derrick (a structure that looks like the Blackpool Tower) As we drew closer, two gigantic cranes were resting in their cradles like sleeping giants. I learnt later that this was a safety precaution so that the crane's jib ('boom') would not collide with the helicopter blades. The chopper began to descend onto a big net, spread and secured to the helideck. This prevented the helicopter from moving when stationary. The landing was soft and pleasant, but the crew advised us to watch out for the rotor blades as we disembarked. They guided us towards what looked like a ship's wheelhouse. Once we were inside, we had to remove our survival suits and any other equipment whilst carrying our bags.

Once clear of the deck the helicopter returned to Aberdeen. I then had to report to the rig master and from there I signed on to the ship's articles (terms and articles) just as I had done when at sea. He instructed me to go down to the storeroom to collect more of my working gear: boots, hybrid jacket, boiler suit and hardhat. The rig master then introduced the boatswain ('bosun') who gave me a tour of the rig and the accommodation. He later showed me where my cabin was and where I would spend the next fortnight's tour of duty. Jim the bosun was a bit of a character – a Scouser and a good man who had spent many years at sea just like myself so we got on well from day one.

'G'wed there larr', he would intone in his dense accent and he put me wise to working offshore, including how to get the most out of my two-week stint.

By now, it was lunchtime so we made our way to the messroom, which was enormous. I had a quick scan to assess the food offerings, which to my delight looked like a five-star hotel menu. It was far superior to the grub I had eaten at sea. I did not know where to start. I wanted it all. I began with the soup, then the main course with a substantial steak, potatoes, veg and tons of fruit. This was a dream come true. I thought I had gone to hell and woken up in heaven. After lunch, Jim the bosun said it was time for me to have 'the tour' of the rig's layout. It was a cold, blustery day so I had to wear my bulky high-viz coat and hardhat, all mandatory once outside the accommodation. As a newbie and being very naïve, I stepped out on deck without my chinstrap secured. A gust of wind lifted the hat from my head and like a flying saucer; it went hurtling over the side of the platform - not a good start!

The rig itself was enormous, like a factory with a multitude of people working in many different departments. I had yet to walk around and look at the drill floor and all the drilling equipment to try and understand the layout of the rig. Some of the crew who I had seen in the mess earlier were barely recognisable; their bodies and clothing were full of mud. They resembled coal miners who had been working down the pit on the coalface for weeks. The rig was moving and lurching from side to side.

It was a 'semi-submersible' drilling platform, which meant that giant anchors secured it to the seabed. This rig could be towed to any new location once it was in the designated area for drilling.

Supply boats would arrive and transport the huge anchors which were then dropped to the sea floor. There would be marker buoys deployed to mark the area where they lay, this would be so that when the rig moved on to another location they would be easily found and the process would start over again. Once the rig has rested in its location, it is submerged to a pre-determined depth to start drilling. Then all eight anchors are heaved taut by winches which are located at each corner of the rig.

Jim took me onto the crane deck where the helicopter refuelling tanks were stored, noting that it was our job to check the fuel daily to ensure it was not contaminated. If the fuel was polluted by residue, it could not be used. This made me apprehensive as these inspections entailed a lot of responsibility but it was one of my key duties. We had a stroll around the rig and Jim explained to me that the maintenance was down to us and if any seamanship ropes or wires were damaged or broken, they would have to be repaired by us just as would happen on a ship.

After a day absorbing my new world, I returned exhausted to my cabin, then into the communal bathroom where I had a shower and changed. Once again, it was back to the messroom for another slap-up meal, after which I discovered the cinema room and the library, which were both spacious with lots of recreational projects to pass the evenings away. As for the pay, it was a significant improvement from my seafaring days. Big money could be earned from working in the drilling department. I intended to investigate working on the drill floor, and the opportunity to earn big bucks later...

This first tour of duty flew by and I was looking forward to seeing my wife and two kids back home. I received a generous allowance for a return flight from Aberdeen to Manchester for each trip which was intended to cover the highest airfares with leading carriers. I soon learnt from others that there were potentially great savings to be made by using alternative means of travel including using my own car to drive the long distance to and from Aberdeen. This proved to be a mixed blessing as it was a very arduous road journey, added to the fact that returning home from the rig after working for most of the morning before crew change day was in itself very tiring. Once I had settled into the routine of commuting, I therefore investigated alternative and cheaper public transport options such as the train and coach network. These apparently attractive alternatives were, however, not completely risk free because the company paid us to use the airlines for a quick and reliable way of getting us to our allocated crew change slot. Stern questions were asked if we failed to turn up for the helicopter flight out to the rig on crew change day. The 'culprit' would have to explain why the allocated airfares had not been spent and this infraction could have resulted in instant dismissal from the company. I did manage to save some money in the five years with the company, but not without a few very close calls when trying to make the deadline for crew change shifts.

It was mandatory to attend several offshore courses paid for by my employer. The first was an essential survival course at a training centre in Aberdeen. I was just into the start of my second week's leave when I received a phone call from the personnel department informing me that my first training course would commence at the end of my leave. The duration was Monday to Friday. I would spend the weekend in the hotel in Aberdeen before re-joining my rig the following Monday morning. I travelled up north on the Sunday morning (by coach - another few quid in my pocket!). After alighting at Aberdeen bus station at around 5pm, I checked into the Skean-Dhu Dyce just in time for my evening meal. After my tasty feast, I went to the bar, scanning the room for anybody who might be on the course. There were a couple of guys who I recognised from previous tours on the rig so we shared a few stories, then after a few bevvies it was time to turn in.

The following morning after breakfast, we convened outside. A minicab driver took us to the nearby training centre which did not look too frightening from the outside considering what was in store for us all. After reporting in at reception, we went into the changing room where we received our kit and instructions regarding what lay ahead over the next few days. We just looked at each other in despair. A couple of training officers dressed in uniforms greeted us: one who looked like a bull terrier: the other short, stocky and surly. Neither inspired confidence. They briefed us on what to expect. Day one was to be spent in the pool learning how to launch and use the inflatable life raft. This process involved jumping from a diving board, fully kitted up with a boiler suit and heavy work boots topped by a survival suit worn on top. As we lined up and walked reluctantly towards the pool's side, we resembled a line of convicts dressed in orange overalls. The only thing that was missing was the ball and chain.

The 'bull terrier' instructed us to enter the water one by one. I walked towards the steps that led into the water. As my feet became submerged, I hesitated for a second before lowering my heavily kitted body into the freezing water. (It was a good job I learnt to swim a little.) After we were all submerged, shouts came from somewhere near the diving board ordering us to climb out, proceed to the board steps and to climb to the top. This was daunting and frightening, as I had never jumped into water from any great height. Now that my kit was soaking wet, it weighed twice as much as it did dry. As I neared the edge of the board whilst holding onto the rail, I took one quaking look down. From below, the diving board did not look very high but now that I was at the top, it the pool seemed very small and infinitely far away.

'Ok – you're next!' the command barked out, 'on you go - jump laddie, jump!'

It was now or never. I froze. Looking down once more, I teetered on the edge then just dropped myself into the pool.

Once I had swam to the surface, the big man was at the edge of the pool gesturing at me to swim towards the other end where the life raft was floating upside down. Its swollen, circular, outer rubber body loomed out of the water like a bloated carcass and hanging from it were some grab ropes, which were to be grabbed in the event of the raft capsizing. After finally reaching the far end of the pool, my body was already aching and tired after what felt like a swim the width of the English Channel. After constantly sliding back into the water, I eventually hauled my aching limbs onto the craft and simultaneously tried to swim on my back, hauling the life raft along with me. I could not grab hold of it from below because it was like trying to gain a grip on the skin of a wet whale. Happily, two guys then swam to help me by clinging onto the raft and back paddling in the water. Unfortunately, this took the monster under the freezing water because of the weight of our clothes and boots. To compound our misery, the instructors began firing cold water onto us with huge fire hoses. We were only allowed to climb out of the pool once we had righted this giant, and by now, we all had had enough. After our evening meal, a few beers and a bit of banter followed by a few laughs, it was off to get some well-earned kip. However, there was worse to come the following day.

Day two of the course turned out to be the worst day so far. The training pertained to escaping from an upturned capsule. The exercise prepared us for potentially ditching from a helicopter at sea. A capsule (representing the chopper) was lowered and submerged into the freezing water from an overhead crane. When we were inside, it rotated to 180° until we were upside down. We were told to hold our breaths and count up to seven seconds before releasing the seat belt and swimming for the escape exit. Those seven, long seconds felt like a lifetime. I tried to unbuckle my belt but my fingers were too numb to release the catch. I finally managed by tugging frantically at the release mechanism. The added stress made me want to hyperventilate but it was imperative to hold my breath. Now it was time to make my way towards the exit, which proved very difficult, as I had to find my way around the edges of the window frame where the glass had been removed. I pulled myself through bit by bit, until I was clear. I could not hold my breath for much longer but to my horror; my feet caught in the exit on the way out. Oh my god, this is it. If I get stuck, I won't be able to swim out! I crawled the rest of the way towards the ladder with my life jacket in tow and my boots, which had doubled in weight since the morning. I managed to grab hold of one rung then I just hauled my aching body onto the slippery tiles.

By day three, I was full of dread and trepidation. We reported to reception, and then filed into the changing room. I was not looking forward to this. I think my hands were frost- bitten. Once again, I changed into a dry boiler suit, boots and hardhat. I made my way towards the edge of the pool where the instructors were waiting for us impassive and professional, but to my jaundiced eyes like predatory wolves fletching their teeth.

'Morning, sir, my teeth are still grinding together from the cold yesterday!'

'Morning, LADDIE.'

'I believe we're in for it today, Sir?'

'Oh, yes, you certainly are,' he glinted back.

I lowered my aching limbs into the water as the other guys appeared in my wake. One of them seemed to be still suffering from the cold and could have even been hypothermic. This was our final day in the pool, the other couple of days we could just do whatever we wanted to. So, there were no more tricks thrown at us. We were told to swim from one end to the other until we could not go on any longer. By this time, we could only manage a couple of slow lengths before we were totally exhausted. I think that the trainers knew that we had all genuinely reached the limits of endurance. They instructed us to proceed to the showers and change into dry warm clothing. That was all for this course. We would now receive our confirmation certificate.

The first course was now over and done with so it was time to go back to working offshore. I felt as though I had settled in well on this platform. It was now time for me to research and investigate the workings of the drill floor on this rig.

I had learned that qualifications were not required to progress to each level in the drilling and exploration aspects of the oil or gas industry. I had also been told that this kind of work was only for 'young men' and not for someone thirty years old like me. However, one thing I had learned from my childhood and my later years was that nothing comes easy without hard work and determination along with the will to succeed in anything we set out to do.

I decided to discuss my intentions of working on the drill floor with the bosun, whom I respected. He warned me that it would be a big mistake to move into the drilling division. He noted that I was too old, and that it was a job suited to a younger generation. I listened to him, but the inner Alan would never give up on up an opportunity like this. I explored what drilling work entailed in more detail. I never had a chance as a child to get on in life or improve myself. So now, for the first time, I spotted an opportunity and a challenge. I could be making the biggest mistake of my life, but every time I walked up to the drill floor and talked to the guys, I received good feedback and positive vibes. It had been around six months since I first started working on this rig. Now was the time to make my move into the drilling department. I had a chat with the head of operations who was the tool pusher. I had already seen him about and had a bit of a rapport with him. I went along to his office and put my idea to him that I would like to change over from the seamen's crew and move into the drill crew. We had a bit of banter together and a good laugh. He said he would not stand in my way and would offer me a position as soon as there was a vacancy within any of the drilling crews. I would start at the bottom, as this is how it worked, operating as a 'roustabout' at the bottom of the pile. I noted to him that I might be too old to take on this role. He laughed, 'never too old laddie!' So, this was finally it. I would finally get the chance to prove myself and confound all the doubters.

Once I had a place within a drill crew, I had to inform the bosun and the barge master that I had secured a position and would not be returning to the seamen's crew. The bosun, however, had already heard through the grapevine that I had asked for a change over to the drilling. Having heard the news second-hand and not from me, I could tell he was not impressed. Up to this point, I had got on well with the barge master but now the relationship went downhill. He told me that he would have liked to have heard it from me first as per protocol which reinforced the constant reminders from the bosun that I should have spoken with the barge master about my intentions. My tardiness in letting them both know therefore left me feeling unsettled and unhappy before I had even made the move over to the other side. From then on, every time I met the barge master either on or off the rig, he would just walk past me without saying 'hello'. He was a nice guy; I just went about it in the wrong way. The damage had now been well and truly done, so I had to move forward and make my move, as there was no going back now. I did one more trip as seaman, and then I was informed that I would join a crew as a roustabout. Yes, yes! This was my chance, my one and only chance I had to go for it!

I met my new crew in the hotel the night before crew change. They seemed a rowdy bunch. Many of them were young, so I just took notes of what was going on. I kept myself to myself for a while. After a night's sleep, it was time to head off to the heliport. Once I arrived on the rig, I bumped into the barge master who never spoke but just gave me a sad look. I made my way down into the accommodation; I was sharing a room with two of the other roustabouts on the crew. One of them seemed to be a cocky little swine, and he looked me up and down. After our meal, we made our way out on deck to take up our duties.

The crane driver on a rig was the boss of all the roustabouts - like a supervisor you could say. He was a Geordie who had a bit of a mouth on him - another cocky swine! As the first shift got underway, we had to get some drill pipe ready for sending up to the drill floor. This was one of my jobs now working in this crew. I felt out of place, I also felt sad that certain people looked upon me as if I had betrayed them and let them down. My decision was made and I had to persevere. I had witnessed so many people in my life who had worked hard to make something of themselves. It had been a long time coming, but I felt as though this was my time. It was not just about me moving on, but it was an excellent opportunity to earn good money so that my family could have some good things in life. I was not afraid to get my hands dirty; I was not frightened of hard work; this is how I was brought up in a big family living almost in poverty. With no formal qualifications from my school days, through no fault of my own, I looked upon this as a chance to make something of my life.

My working hours were from 1200 to 2400 then it was shower time, supper and bed. Same thing - day in, day out, until the first week was over. On the following Monday we began our second and last week. We changed shift on that day for just four hours, then had a few hours off before heading to bed. Too soon, it was up again at 23.00 to start 12-hour nights. The second Monday was always the change of shift day. I never got much sleep on this day and I was never keen on working nights, but this was how it worked as the rig operated twenty-four/seven. I did not feel comfortable in this crew, because I didn't seem to fit in. The crane driver, who seemed to run the team, did not appear to have much time for me. I am not sure why; maybe he thought I was too old, and they looked upon me as a joke - but I knew differently! Anyway, the fortnight passed; I went home and had my two weeks leave. Then it was back again with the same crew. My instinct was right; I had been placed with a crew with whom I wasn't one of their club members. This was very unfortunate because I could not prove myself.

The North Sea was a cold and windy environment to work in. If there was not much drilling going on, we just plodded on with maintenance. Some jobs had to be done, like cleaning and painting inside storerooms down in the main legs of the rig which at least got you out of the cold. However, I never seemed to be delegated the cushy numbers that consistently went to the favourites and didn't they know it! When we had our breaks, I would arrive back inside cold and wet. They, on the other hand, were warm and dry with gloating smirks that never failed to piss me off. This of course exacerbated my plight. Word started to get around that I did not fit in with this crew.

I knew if the crane driver had any say in the decision (and he did!) I was not in the running order to get the next position on the floor. I went out of my way to try and get on the good side of the crane driver. But he wasn't having any of it. So, the only way that I was going to find out the reason why he had no time for me was to confront him about my concerns.

But I knew that I was running the risk of making a fool of myself. Then the opportunity came when he asked me to wash down the crane that he had just finished driving.

'Hey do you mind If I have a word in confidence?' I asked.

'Sure, what's on your mind?'

'To be honest. I feel as though you don't like me for some reason. But I don't know what I am supposed to have done wrong to upset you'

'Howay man calm doon, are yee daft?'

'I wish I knew but whenever I try to have a chat, you just seem to just look at me and walk away.'

'No man, get owa yeh self, and wash the fukin crane dee as ya telt. Are yee fukin daft?'

Being isolated on a platform, there was always gossip and everybody seemed to know each other's business. It was like a little village in the middle of nowhere. After a two-week tour of duty, it was time to head off home via Aberdeen. On one occasion when I travelled home by train, there were some of my crew on the same journey. They seemed to be having a good booze-up, but I was not one of them. I got the occasional few grunts and smirks before being sent on my way so I kept myself to myself. Once I arrived home after the very long trip, I was tired and the next day I was just glad to be home again with my family. Still, my wife made a comment that I did not look happy and asked whether I had had a bad two weeks.

'No,' I said, 'I am fine just tired,' But that was not true. When you have lived with somebody for over twenty years, it is difficult to hide your feelings. After two days, I just tried to switch off and enjoy my leave. Then a couple of days before it was time to return, my mood seemed to change again to sadness. I dismissed this sense of foreboding because it was only early days and I had to look to the future.

On the train back to Aberdeen for my second tour of duty with this crew, I reflected on the excellent job I had once had as a seaman and asked myself repeatedly whether I had made a colossal mistake. I dismissed the negative thoughts because it was early days and I had to look to the future. I was determined to one day make it big and show everybody that I was capable of rising above all the comments and the negativity that was coming my way.

The crew met up in the hotel bar the night before crew change. After checking in, I made my way through the dining room to join them. I recognised some of the guys from my crew and knew they could see me coming. As I approached I said, 'Hi, how are you all doing? Have you had a good leave?' I was just trying to break the ice.

The reply comprised a few grunts and not much else so I knew that I was in for another miserable two weeks. One or two people tried to initiate some conversation but they were not part of the drill crew. After a few beers, I made my way to my room that I shared. My sleep was disturbed because my mind was playing tricks on me, overthinking and plaguing me with questions like why am I here, what have I done? However, I was here to stay, so just kept my head down and worked hard to get to where I wanted to be and to hell with everybody else.

The next morning after breakfast, it was time to board the minibus for the short, ten-minute run out to the heliport in Dice. Once there, it was the same rigorous routine; security was alert to anybody who looked worse for wear with drink. It was unfortunate for me that I was in a crew with whom I did not get on. I had to get to know the driller because it would be his decision as to who would get the next available roughnecks' job, but he knew all about me from the crane driver, who would have stabbed me in the back and put an end to my dream of progressing to a higher level. I knew before too long that I would have to confront him about his unreasonable behaviour towards me.

After a couple more trips out on the rig, I got to know the guys who worked on the floor. The crew comprised three roughnecks, one derrick man, an assistant driller and the lead driller. I made a point of spreading the word around amongst these guys that I was interested in working on the floor. I introduced myself to the driller and informed him of my intentions to progress into drilling. He was a young Yorkshire man who was pleasant and hardworking, and said that when the opportunity presented itself, he would give me an initial chance to relieve the roughnecks for their breaks. By doing this, he would see how I worked. Now that I had got to know this man, it wasn't too long before he called for me to relieve the lads on the floor. I was very excited at the prospect of working on the sharp end of the job. My first opportunity came and I had to do my best to impress. They called me up to take my place with the other two roughnecks. I had already observed how they worked. I soon realised however, that watching is nothing like the actual involvement and technique that the crew performed while drilling was in full swing. It took three men and a derrick man to work the drilling operations. The driller had already noticed that I had shown a very strong interest in the work. He called me over to the 'doghouse' (where the driller works and operates the machinery and controls that, in turn, operate the drilling equipment in the derrick, on the drill floor, and the mudroom.)

The mudroom is where particles from the drilled hole are pumped back up to the mudroom where the debris is separated from the reusable mud, which then circulates back down the drill pipe to the drill bit. The mud is made up from powder chemicals that start their journey via the mudroom, it was the job of the derrickman to mix the chemicals. This reusable mud is used to keep the drilled hole lubricated as well as cleaning and cooling the head of the drill bit. Any waste is returned back into the sea. The driller told me I would soon relieve the men on the floor more often. I was excited but also nervous at the prospect of working in such a wet, cold and dangerous environment. Nonetheless, I had to take this opportunity to prove to myself that nothing and nobody would stand in my way of achieving my goals in life. A few days passed before the decision was made for me to relieve the men on the floor. As I made my way up the slippery steel stairway that led to the working area, I was shaking as my nerves had got the better of me. I could hear the motors and the grinding of the equipment as I got nearer to the actual location of drilling. The roughnecks were barely recognisable with mud spattered over their entire bodies. The driller called me over to the doghouse that had steel horizontal bars across the window area. I guess they were there to stop any equipment that broke loose from smashing through into it. I could not hear what he was trying to say to me, but I could understand his directions and body language enough to make my way towards one of the roughnecks and watch them at work for a few minutes before taking over from one of them. As I relieved the roughneck, I tried to mirror what he was doing. Teamwork was vital in a three-man crew involved in a very dangerous job. It was like synchronised engineering -each and every one of us had a role to play otherwise things could have gone badly wrong.

At the time of my taking over, we were 'tripping the pipe'. This meant bringing all the drill pipe up from the sea then through the centre of the platform and the rotary table hole where we inserted slips. These acted like a wedge to hold the drill pipe in place, while they split the two joints, ready for the derrick man to rack the stand back high above the drill floor. This was a very dangerous job, because he was located high up on the derrick and had to walk out onto what we know as a 'monkey board'. One day I would have to do this, I thought. The tongs (giant mechanical spanners) were very heavy and needed to be manoeuvred around the pipe. While a roughneck put one tong around the lower joint of pipe, another roughneck would put the other tong around the top joint. This was a bit like using two wrenches to tighten a joint together, or vice versa to dismantle the pipes, but the drill pipes were huge and made out of thick steel. The driller in the doghouse worked the controls to tension both tongs up (with the wires leading from the end), which were then tightened by the winches. At the same time, both roughnecks had to ensure that the tongs fitted onto the drill joints so they could grip. If a tong slipped, it could cause the roughnecks to catch their hands, which could cause severe injuries. During my short time on the rig, I witnessed many individuals leave the floor with injuries whilst working and tripping over pipes, along with other hazards of operating on a moving platform. I was always mindful that

I could fall victim to an accident, so I had to be constantly on my guard and learn as much as I could to keep my mates and myself safe.

Once I actually got stuck into the routine of working with the lads, I started to relax and enjoy what I was doing. The two roughnecks I was working with seemed to take me under their wing, and ensured that I was working safely, not just only for myself but for those who worked alongside me. The feedback I got over the next couple of days regarding my short time on the floor was very positive. It led me to believe that I must have impressed the driller and the crew, which boosted my enthusiasm to a higher level.

Now I knew that it would not be long before the opportunity would arise again for me to do more relieving up top. Within a few days, I was again asked to relieve one of the roughnecks. This time my job was a little different, but I was still working as a team of three. Towards the end of another gruelling twelve-hour shift, I returned down onto the deck with the other roustabouts and crane driver. This hurtled me back down to earth. Despite my hopes being raised, it felt as though nothing had changed. I still got all the shit jobs and did not fit in. This seemed a shame now that I had had my first relief with the crew. However, after my fourth trip with this team I was getting plenty of experience relieving the drill floor. Despite everything, I was becoming increasingly self-confident and comfortable with the tasks I had to do. I think this irritated the crane driver and the other roustabouts; I just seemed to be proving them wrong. I knew if the crane driver had any say in the decision (and he did!) I was not in the running order to get the next position on the floor. Sometimes I would bump into the bosun who I had worked with for a while in the seaman's crew. He would give me the once over, but the look on his face said it all. I could read his mind. He did not say much to me but I knew what he was thinking. There were, however, many occasions when I admittedly had reservations about my choices and decisions regarding the transfer to drilling. I could not always be 'looking through my rear-view mirror' otherwise I would not get anywhere in life. I had just been unlucky to have been part of an immature crew. I just felt fortunate that somebody had faith in me and had given me the opportunity to move on.

Working down on the main decks was also a very hazardous place to be. It involved working with the crane operator and giving him directions where to lift and land equipment for example, oxygen bottles for the welder. In addition, numerous obstacles on deck and other hidden areas created blind spots obstructing our views on deck. This, together with the movement of the rig and bad weather, made it difficult to negotiate walking on top of wet and slippery pipes and steel casing. It was very hazardous. All the above challenges were exacerbated when working on the night shift along with the hazards of the motion of the rig moving about on the North Sea. My two weeks' tour of duty sometimes went quickly. I did occasionally miss the good times that I had enjoyed when I was deep sea. That life had been great, even though the pay was not! It was the freedom of the sea without any worries but in my current role, it was just work, rest and no play. I persevered, however, motivated by the welfare of my wife and two children.

I had now completed many tours of duty on this rig and with this crew. To this day I do not recall how it came about that I was offered a permanent position within the drill crew and it took me by surprise, considering the prior attitude of the backstabbing crane driver and undermining my ability to progress. I could not turn this opportunity down to be made officially a roughneck. Word got around about my promotion and I hoped that it would reach the people who doubted me. The weeks and months went by working on the floor and I steadily became more knowledgeable about drilling. It must have been about four months into the job when things started to go wrong. It began when I had an accident whilst clamping the tongs around the joints of the drill pipe. If the tongs did not bite (grip) around the joints of the pipes, they would slip and that meant that we had to get a firm grasp on the handles of the tongs. Our fingers were consequently vulnerable and could collide with the other tong that operated by another roughneck. Precisely this happened to me, and as a result, I cut one of the fingers on my right hand. It obviously needed stitching. There was a first-aider on the rig who was a medic but with limited skills below those of a nurse or doctor. He put some stitches in my finger, which resembled a piece of old canvas being patched up on a ship's sail. It did the job however and I was sent straight back to work on the floor.

There was no mercy on this job, and sympathy was in short supply as we were out in the North Sea moving about on a huge steel platform, just like a bouncy castle on the high seas. The day I injured my hand, I was on my lunch break. The driller sat opposite me while I was eating but there was no conversation between us. He just glanced in my direction and did not say a word. Not only did I continue to feel pain but I could see the blood seeping through my already damp and wet muddy gloves. The more pressure I put on it while using the tongs, the more blood dripped down my hand. I knew that my crewmates were aware of my discomfort when I returned back from lunch and that they could see the blood. One of them called out to the driller who then called me over so he could have a look. He suspended the tripping out of the hole of the drill pipe and called on the PA for one of the roustabouts to come up and relieve me. When the relief arrived on the drill floor, I went down to the tool pushers' office to the medic. I peeled away my sodden glove that stuck painfully to my damaged finger. My wound was severe. The medic attempted to clean the affected area, which caused me much pain. The blood was still seeping out. He told me I would need to go ashore to Aberdeen Hospital and have the wound stitched and attended to properly. This did not go down very well with the tool pusher who was also present. The radio officer made a call to Aberdeen for a repatriation helicopter to take me ashore. There was none available, so a helicopter had to be diverted to our rig to transport me ashore where I was driven to the hospital.

The waiting time in the hospital was around two to three hours. It required about four stitches after the poor pathetic crude thread was removed that the medic had to use to patch me up, and some bandaging was applied before I was discharged. From there I had to make my own way to Aberdeen train station and begin my long, sad journey home. I called my wife to relay the bad news and that I would be returning home later that evening. It was a sad and lonely journey as I started to reflect on the accident and what impact it would have on my future, along with the implications for my career plans working on the floor with this crew. I arrived home around 8pm after a 9-hour journey. I was not feeling well from the injury but the hospital had supplied me with some painkillers and told me to report to my local GP. The following morning, I phoned the company and was given a sick note for a month, although I did not intend to stay off work that long. As the days went by and my finger started to heal, I went to see the nurse and she removed the stitches. The wound looked bruised and swollen but I was determined to get back for my next crew change. I spoke to the personnel department who were very understanding.

Being at home set me mulling over the setback and raised the old regrets about my decision to move from the seamen crew into the drilling. I would always have these doubts at the back of my mind when things were not going right for me. My wound healed quickly and I soon re-joined my crew. As usual, we met in the hotel the night before we flew out to the installation. Just like every other time on the night before crew change, I had my evening meal in the hotel, then headed for the bar to socialise with the guys. As ever, I still did not feel welcome so my morale was at an all-time low. I also did not sleep too well that night. It must have been around 2 or 3am the following morning when my roommate opened the door and made a point of slamming it shut, he then staggered to his bed, I guessed that this was his 'unwelcome back' gesture!

During the two-hour flying time to the platform, I tried to sleep but could not with the rotor blades pulsing and chopping into my already anxious thoughts. I closed my eyes and started thinking what I would be facing in a couple of hours' time with all the comments from my ex-bosun. I dreaded to think what some of the crew would have been saying about me when I left the rig after my accident, especially the fat-bellied crane driver with his red, spotty face!

The weather was foul with freezing, blustery winds and heavy sleet cascading down onto the rig with great force. There was an area on deck where drill pipes and other equipment would be sent down onto the deck with great force. It was very important to be aware and mindful of what could be coming down from the floor to avoid any serious accidents. Whilst walking on the main deck one cold, blustery night, I stepped across the catwalk situated at the bottom of the drill floor. This acted like a huge steel shoot for equipment and drill pipes being sent back down after use. All heavy equipment was lifted by crane to and from the floor. On this particular night, a section of pipe was launched down from the floor and came cascading down without any prior word from above. Nobody looked down or even checked to see if there was anybody at the bottom. Unfortunately, that 'anybody' happened to be me. As I stepped over the catwalk, I did not have enough time to dodge the huge chunk of steel. The pipe ricocheted against the side ledge and trapped my foot between the steel and the drill pipe. This, in turn, damaged my right foot, and I was in a lot of pain. After close examination, I could not see any visible cuts or bleeding, but there was a lot of very painful bruising around the side of my foot. This time, in light of my accident history, I decided not to report this particular incident. I had made so many claims for damages and it would also involve loss of earnings. At the time, I was working alone on the deck so nobody else would have known or witnessed my accident. I was grateful for this small mercy. I found a quiet secluded location inside one of the lockers situated in the huge legs of the rig. After further inspecting my injury, I became increasingly concerned for the damage I might potentially have done to my foot.

This latest mishap did not help my anxiety levels. I did not want anybody to know because word would get around that (yet again) I had had another accident. I could not hide my pain as I was limping around the deck. I know I should have gone along to see the medic but I could not bring myself to do this again. I felt ashamed. I had been on the rigs for a few years and had brought all this trauma on myself through the mistake I had made changing from seamen's crew to the drill crew. Despite the intense pain, I still had about eight hours of my shift to go before I finished. Every time I pressed my foot further into my boot, every step I took, I just felt pain - real pain to an extent that I had never experienced before. I just did not know what to do, but I soldiered on because I could not report it. After gathering some old white rags from the box that was left open in the store, I waited until breaktime then went into the bathroom and soaked the rags into cold water. I was not sure what I was doing but I knew I had to get the swelling down. At the same time, I had to make sure that nobody was watching me. I applied the cold makeshift bandage and the cold went through my entire body. I managed it to the end of the shift and without anybody knowing about my accident. I did not dare go into the dining room because there were so many people and I was certain to be noticed limping around. I had a shower, limped my way towards my cabin, climbed into my bunk and lay there trembling with cold and pain. I tried to position my leg so that it would not hang over the edge of the bunk, just in case my roommate happened to knock it. I was worried about the damage to my foot and any long-term internal injury.

I managed to get through the next couple of trips without injuries. It must have been during early months when it went awry for me again with yet another accident on my already damaged right hand. This is when I realised that I had another problem with my fellow crewmates on the floor. Due to the cacophony from all the machinery, it was very difficult to communicate with one another. I felt as though I was not keeping up with what was being said to me concerning my part of the work as a team. I thought I might have some hearing problem. I had not been aware of this before; maybe I just had to get accustomed to the noise and work with it like the others did. It was not long before a couple of roughnecks told me that I needed to 'put more effort' into what I was doing because I was not keeping up with the rhythm of tripping the pipe and all the other jobs on the floor. My confidence started to spiral downwards along with my self-assurance. I was now in a vicious circle of being fearful of having more accidents, which in turn had a profound impact on my sleeping patterns.

When I returned home for my fortnight's leave, I spoke once again with my wife and we made the decision that it was time for me to accept defeat, write to the company and ask them for a transfer to either another crew or another platform. I did not hear from them for a while but just before departure for my tour of duty, I received a crushing letter from HR. It stated that if I wanted a rig transfer, I would have to wait for a vacancy. In the interim, I had been 'demoted' to roustabout and had to return to my normal crew change. The letter did not explain why they had demoted me, but it did not take much figuring out. Two days before my scheduled return I received a second phone call from personnel who informed me that I would also change to another rig, operated by Houlder Marine, also based in the North Sea. This meant returning one week earlier, so that I could pick up the crew change with my new team.

I returned to Aberdeen in July 1985 after working offshore for about four years. Again, trying to save the difference on my flight allowance, I used the train. I was not sure with whom I would be crewing up on this installation. There was the usual routine on the night before flying out and some of my new crew assured me in the hotel bar that this crew were a 'great bunch' of lads. I felt more relaxed than on previous occasions and had a sense of wellbeing with these men. At least I could try (as a demoted roughneck!) to make a fresh start. Nevertheless, I was very apprehensive about opening up too much until I got to know them better. The rig I was about to join was identical to the one I had just left. I relieved the crew who were on the second week of their tour of duty. Although the first few hours of the shift seemed to go okay with my co-workers/colleagues, it was difficult to accept my lowlier status. I felt as though my world had fallen apart, just as everyone had told me it would. I had to learn to swallow my pride and try to put past setbacks behind me. In practice, this was not easy, as occasionally during a crew change, people from other rigs were transferred to my new platform for promotional reasons, and they loved to spread gossip and rumours. Still, after the first couple of days, I seemed to hit it off with the lads. I was able to make them laugh and they welcomed someone new as they had worked together for some time. Even my sleep seemed to have improved and I was not worried about accidents as I had been on the other rig.

The crane driver (a southerner), seemed to be an easy-going sort, in total contrast to the last backstabber that I had worked with. I just felt so relaxed, but I asked myself whether this new self-belief was just due to my not being on the drill floor anymore. Still, I had regained self-respect along with a little dignity. There seemed to be no more backstabbing like there was before. I could not help thinking that this should have been the crew I worked with in the first place — again it was all down to the luck of the draw! Ironically, but just like before, my sleep patterns continued to worsen and in retrospect I think I was heading for a period of depression and anxiety. This was in total contrast from when I had been at sea and was always relaxed. Life was easy then with no worries and no pressure. There were terrible thoughts going through my head, which haunted me and niggled at my consciousness. I plagued myself asking whether I had made a huge mistake. Not only was the decision I made to changing over to the drill crew haunting me, but my negativity was also compounded by often bumping into the barge master who I first met when I joined the rigs. He remained hurt and offended due to me not consulting him about my move. The insomnia, anxiety and depression that I was experiencing started to have a dramatic impact on my personality and mood. I was reluctant to seek GP support at home because the reports that would ensue might make their way back to the company which I did not think would be a good idea.

I was now settled in with this new crew as a roustabout and everything seemed to be going okay. I just had to get on with it and avoid further accidents, which could happen because the work was similar to what happened on the drill floor, using the same equipment. Added pressure came from working away and leaving my wife to bring up two young children. I consoled myself by trying to do the best I could for my family. I also knew that my job at sea would not last forever, so I felt as though I had to move over to the oil industry when the opportunity presented itself. There were rewards working offshore, but again it all depended on what skills an individual possessed. I was becoming very concerned about my mental health and wellbeing. I had heard about people who suffer from anxiety seeking professional help or counselling, but I was reluctant to go down that road.

By the start of the late 1980s, I was earning more money than I had done at sea and wanted to put it to good use. It had always been my intention to buy my own home. However, I was not earning enough money to purchase a good sized house in the private sector. Our house then was a three-bedroom semi-detached council house. The Conservative Party was in power and in 1980, Margaret Thatcher introduced the right to buy scheme for council house tenants who had a good rent payment record.

This enabled tenants to buy their home from the local council at a discounted rate. I engaged a solicitor to advise me where to apply for and what to do about a mortgage. Considering it was a council house, it was quite a generous size. I knew that there was potential for improving the property as it also had space for a driveway and a garage leading to the garden. After consulting a mortgage advisor, I applied to the council for the purchase of the property but like anything involving the council there was no rush. After an interminable wait, we received council confirmation granting us permission to purchase. Happily, we would qualify for a generous discount because of the lengthy period that we had been tenants of the property so after about twelve months, we finally became homeowners.

Now that the waiting was over, I could work on turning the house into our own home. Because it was an ex-council house, everything was basic. It had no central heating; both the window frames and the kitchen needed renovating.

A few months later, the house was looking good with new windows, new kitchen and central heating. I would rather be paying a mortgage than paying rent for the rest of my life. It really was an achievement that I felt proud of and it was proof of the positive results of working hard and being able to achieve whatever you set your mind to – a lesson I tried to teach my children.

At last I owned my own property, which gave me sense of achievement, no more waiting for the local council to make shoddy repairs then going on to increase our weekly payments to pay for the work done. This made me very optimistic for the future. The house represented positive progress after about two years working offshore with all my difficulties and setbacks. It encouraged me that I could still improve my lifestyle and that of my family. Part of this included family holidays together in sunny climes so we had several vacations in Spain. However, I wanted something more permanent so I carried out some research into buying a time-share or 'fractional ownership' property as they were called at the time. This concept was new then and there were only a few companies offering them.

It was while we were away in Spain that a time-share representative approached us. He handed me some brochures and information sheets regarding apartments in the area where we were on holiday. The property was a modest one-bedroom property with just basic amenities but after several days' consideration, it seemed an attractive proposition. It would provide us with access for one week every year (the apartment was only available in June of each year) for the same apartment and for life. The fee was around £4,000 plus a yearly maintenance charge, which was quite substantial at the time. The agent suggested that if I wanted to go ahead with the deal, I would 'have to be quick' because of high demand for the properties. I contacted my bank and my bank manager agreed to provide the necessary funding for the investment. The total loan was six thousand pounds including interest payments over a three-year period. I telephoned the property agent to inform him that I now had the available funds in place.

We were very excited and could not wait for our first holiday in our very own apartment. After a few days in our new property, we noticed several problems. My wife and I were not impressed. I contacted the company, but they were unhelpful although they promised try to correct the problems.

Time passed and we knew that nothing had been rectified. I contacted them again and asked whether we could upgrade to a better apartment with two bedrooms. This was possible but would have entailed further financial investment and borrowing from the bank. It was beginning to look as though they had conned us with this timeshare. I blamed myself for rushing into it, but in my defence, naïve though it may seem now, I had been led to believe that the apartments were 'selling very quickly' and I had felt pressurised to 'make my move' and sign the contract. I was reluctant to incur more debt. My main concern was whether I would ever be able to re-sell this apartment. After giving it more thought, I decided not to take out any more loans. I kept up with all the payments for around three years at £400 per month. This comprised a substantial outgoing for me on top of providing for my wife and family and mortgage payments. We never returned to the apartment. I investigated whether there were any contract loopholes but there was nothing in my favour. I felt ashamed and ripped off by the developers and their agents and that they had taken me for a fool despite never considering myself as naïve.

It is easy in retrospect to say 'we live and learn' but this was a big financial loss and a big mistake to have made along with all the stress and worry that went with it. I had to continue to honour my payments that included the initial purchase price plus an annual maintenance charge. I sought legal advice, but was informed that I had signed a 'binding agreement' and had to keep up the payments with the bank otherwise my credit rating could be impacted. Despite this advice, I eventually cancelled all payments for the maintenance. I informed the company that I was withholding maintenance charges because they had reneged on their own commitments to maintain and repair the property. I never heard from them again and never discovered what happened to the apartment. I guess they just re-sold my apartment even though I had some mickey mouse agreement to say the property was mine 'for life'.

Some years after my own bad experience, the government legislated to help people like myself to have more control over these overseas companies taking advantage and conning people. The new laws gave people flexibility, a lengthy cooling down period and mandatory legal rights for the purchaser to change their mind within a certain time period despite having signed a contract. There was nothing in place like this when I purchased our holiday home. These new regulations did not help my case.

As time passed I grew increasingly unhappy with the way the doctors had stitched my daughter Rachel's cheek injury at the local hospital. She was only eight years old at the time and I was away at sea when she had her accident. I was very upset when I returned home to see the deep scar on her face. It appeared very wide with a deep stretch mark. I expected them to have taken a little more care knowing that she was a young girl who would grow up to be a mature woman. They had however left her with an awareness and permanent reminder through the scar on her face. I was also mindful of the teasing and torments that she might receive from children after school. It bothered me each time I looked at Rachel because she was so young, I tried not to let her see I was looking at her and that it bothered me, but it did very much. As time went by, I tried to monitor her wound without attracting her attention. I did not want her to be paranoid and think that I was always looking, but I was. I had BUPA private medical insurance provided by my company for offshore work but it also offered a discounted rate for family members. I was not sure if the policy would cover restorative surgery. I had hoped to take Rachel to a plastic specialist for surgery to improve the appearance of the scar. My company informed me that I had to talk to my doctor about this, before committing myself to any agreements at this early stage. My doctor was very kind, patient and understanding. He provided a referral to a plastic surgeon specialist in Manchester. After examining Rachel and her wound, the specialist was confident that it would be possible to improve the scar tissue, which would make the area less visible than it was at present. He also informed me that the procedure would be covered by my personal medical insurance. This was great news. However, the process was not without risk. After the surgery, the area around the scar tissue would only be slightly improved from its current appearance. I was concerned about this and asked my wife to take Rachel outside so we could have a personal chat. However, the consultant was adamant that Rachel should be present so that she could hear what was being said. This caused some friction between myself and the consultant but I had to comply with his wishes and ask Rachel to re-enter the room with her mum.

As parents, it was up to my wife and me to make the final decision. The decision was for the surgery to go ahead and it was not too long before Rachel was back at home recovering. They covered the area on her cheek to prevent infection. We had to return to the consultant for him to assess the procedure that he had done on Rachel's check. As time went by her scar seemed to disappear and her beautiful childish looks were once again returning. I could see the change in Rachel's moods. She began to feel more like she was before the tragic accident happened. This also made my wife and I very happy. I took a risk and it paid off. I felt more positive that I had made the right decision to let the consultant perform the plastic surgery on my loving daughter's lovely face, now it was back to work for me.

Working offshore was very hard wet, cold and dirty. It could be very cruel working out in the North Sea. I had been working offshore on both rigs for around about four years by this point. From time to time there were crew changes from one platform to another, as it presented an opportunity for promotion through rotating from one rig to another or covering for other crews who were on leave. I had built up a good working relationship with my crane operator who was also my supervisor. We had got on well together from day one and had great fun working as a team. However, his assistant crane operator was offered the opportunity to work on my previous platform, the Kingsnorth UK, for a two-week tour as a crane operator. This gave him further experience and a foot up the ranking to get a crane operator's job. Something concerned me about this though. I knew people would gossip about me to him while he was on my previous rig. He was just the sort of person who would believe the tales and take it all in. Upon his return, I knew he would open his mouth and spoil everything for me. That would be the end of my happiness on this rig and with this crew. After my leave was over, I returned back to the hotel as usual. Just as I had predicted, he opened his big mouth and at that point I knew what I was in for - some 'slagging' along with the unfounded gossip that he would spread about me.

The next morning when we flew out to join the rig, I could sense the atmosphere. The manner of my crane operator, with whom I had always got on well, was subtly different to how it had been before. After a few days, the gossip about my past started to work its way in the rig news. The person who started all these rumours took great pleasure spreading the word around about my reputation from the other rig. This had a profound effect on how my present crew treated me prior to this person spreading all these lies along with all the reports of the accidents I had had on the other installation. This inevitably damaged my reputation within the team. I had known when this bastard returned to the rig that he would spread the word about me, and was sadly proven right. It was back to square one for me. I could never understand why people had to spread gossip with the sole intent of hurting people. Now the damage had been done.

Meanwhile, life at home was a happy place for me and my family, now that we had Rachel's surgery over and done with, and with a positive outcome. I could see the difference in her happy-go-lucky way of life. She no longer had to dip her head down when she was in the presence of others. This, in turn, made me a happy father and glad that I rolled the dice, and took a huge gamble on our decision to have her surgery re-done.

Returning back to my injured foot. I had been to see the doctor about my foot and he'd arranged for an X-ray. The results were in and I had an appointment for the following day. The news wasn't good. The doctor showed me the X-ray of my injured foot. He tried to explain the inner parts of my injury. I hadn't a clue what all the ghost-like parts of my foot were meant to look like. I think he took pity on my lack of medical knowledge and spared me the anguish of having to ask him what was damaged. He did just that by showing me with a pointer on the X-ray chart. Even though I was none the wiser, he said there was considerable swelling on the ligaments, there's no telling the extent of the injury at this early stage. He just suggested that I continue to rest and try to avoid putting too much pressure on it...

I was now on sick leave AGAIN with self-inflicted injuries. From a psychological point of view, my anxieties and sleep were at an all-time low. I just kept my mind occupied by working on the house renovations as best I could. It was now July 1986 and the oil industry was in decline. Rumours were spreading around Aberdeen when I left the rig to go on leave. The writing was on the wall for most of us, the bubble had burst. People were being laid off. The obvious ones to feel the pinch were the unskilled guys like myself.

After two months on the sick, I received an unwelcome letter from my employers. I was to be made redundant after nearly five years in the offshore industry. This was a big blow to my family and me after having a decent lifestyle for that period. I was, however, given two months' notice, which was a short life-line. I was informed that my rig would now cease operating and would be mothed-balled and lie at anchor somewhere of the Scottish coast.

If I didn't have enough to think about with my injured foot, now a miserable future with no income. I contacted Houlder Marine, and they informed me that the future of the company was very bleak. They told me to stand by and wait for further instructions. A couple of weeks had passed when I received a phone call from HR. They were relocating me to one of their other installations somewhere in the North Sea off the East Coast of England. This was just a one-off tour to assist with the winding down of the rig. After that, I was sent to another semisubmersible (jack-up rig) off the coast of Blackpool. They had a platform working in the gas industry. This was a great job only a fifteen-minute chopper flight from Blackpool Airport. Travelling in Manchester was so accessible by train, just an hour's ride. In total contrast to the long and dreary trip up north. I would have given my right hand to work on this platform, with the close proximity to my home. It felt as though they were giving me a final slap in the face, by dangling a carrot in front of me...

Three weeks later...

The end of my career and any future plans of working offshore had diminished for good. All I ever seemed to think about was what if? Even that dream was now finished. I had been laid-off redundant. Thrown on the scrapheap without any hope for the future. I did, however, receive about a few thousand pounds in severance pay. Now I felt battered and bruised, both mentally and physically. My anxieties and sleepless nights would still show their ugly head. I knew that I was now a full member of the insomniac self-destructive human race. Not a legacy I was proud of. I had learnt some heart-wrenching lessons about both people, and life...

So where did I go from here?

Anxiety and insomnia is what I am left with...

How I yearn for a good night's sleep; what it must be like to lead a normal life, living without the fear of not being able to sleep at night. I usually wake up around the same time every morning at 2 o'clock. No matter what time I go to bed, it always has the same result, just lying there with crazy thoughts churning around inside my head, am I getting a sore throat? Tiredness and anxiety can lead us to lie awake for hours thinking about the things that concern or worry us. The procedure is always the same; I usually rise feeling washed-out which takes its toll on my ability to function during the day. Insomnia can sap not only your energy level and mood, but also your health, work performance and quality of life.

A Pennmedicine.org/news study found that 'about one in four of the population in the United States suffer with insomnia but they recover to sleep normal after a short time. Up to one in four people report difficulty sleeping at least three times a week and the problems are more familiar with older people. Fortunately, it is usually a short-term problem.' When I have been awake for some time, I say to myself.

'Well it will soon be time to make a move,' then I know it is too late even to try and get back to sleep, I just cannot switch off. When I have discussed this with friends and family who have no trouble sleeping, and I see how refreshed they look, they tell me what a good night's sleep they have had, so that upsets me even more. *How can they sleep for so long without even waking just once in the night?* Without the right amount of rest everything becomes twice as difficult to deal with. Even my eating habits are affected. Sometimes it is so difficult to get through the day; one of my quick fixes for the morning is to take a bath to keep myself active for at least another an hour or so.

I have divorced myself from leading a healthy life. However, I have tried using medication, sold over-the-counter from the pharmacist. These were all right for a while but then I found that I had become addicted to them, so they are used as a last resort, for when I really become desperate. Then as the day wears on I will probably end up having another couple of showers, so that I can make it through the rest of the day. I sometimes think that I can cope with the situation, but I know that I am just fooling myself. My social life is non-existent, work becomes a battle. Like most people who have insomnia, I have tried everything from sleeping aids, reading books at night, to having a hot bath before going to bed, (counting sheep) but it is always the same results, waking up after just a couple of hours. Then thinking, here we go again, another long day ahead.

One of the things that affect me the most, is the fact that when I have had a bad night's sleep, I never seem to achieve the things that I have planned for the day, like going to the gym, walking in the park. I usually beat myself up over this for the rest of the day. I feel guilty for not being able to do what I had set out to do. Our bodies need sleep and rest so that we can function throughout the day. I am a member of my local fitness club, so whenever I can drag myself in there, it recharges my batteries for a short while, then I will feel a whole lot better, but the hardest part is finding the motivation to make my body work. However, when I try to work out a daily plan, and hope to achieve the most essential tasks of the week, if there has been a night where 'The Department of Sleep' has allocated me some extra slumber, then that helps for a while. But the problems spill over until the next morning. It would be fair to say that this illness dictates how my life is at present.

Several months had passed after being made redundant... As the saying goes, 'as one door shuts, another opens' and often the clichés are true. I had a lot to think about after leaving the offshore industry. I would find it very difficult to adjust to working ashore and find the right job as I lacked relevant qualifications. Nevertheless, I had a family and a mortgage to pay so I had to find work regardless of the challenges ahead.

CHAPTER FIVE

DRIVING INSTRUCTOR

I eventually became involved with a new start-up driving school. The owners were advertising for fully qualified driving instructors to invest in the business. One criterion was that each instructor had to hold an Advanced Driving Certificate along with an ADR (Approved Driving Instructor) Certificate. However, the more that I researched this new venture, the more I discovered that things were not as straightforward as it first appeared. I learnt belatedly that I wouldn't be receiving a share in the business so I became very suspicious of their motives in potentially trying to con me out of my redundancy pay. I pulled out of the deal before I had signed any contracts, and decided that this was the time to go it alone. After passing part one the theory test of the three-stage driving instructor examinations, it was time to go forward to the next stage which was the driving test. This part was well above the standards of the routine test enabling a member of the public to drive a car on a public road. Once I had passed this second test, I would be able to work for a driving school under licence, which would provide me with the experience to be able to apply for the final part three.

There were two senior examiners at the test centre in Sale, Cheshire, one of them had a reputation as being very strict and 'by-the-book'. He took no prisoners when it came to marking candidates down. After sitting in the test centre waiting room waiting very nervously to take my part two test, a tall man appeared from another room. He looked more like a funeral director than a test examiner. He scoured the cold dark corners of the room and asked in an uncaring manner and a sharp, distinctive voice,

'Mr Alan Whittaker?'

At that moment I knew that he must be the unpopular examiners out of the two.

'Yeeees,' I nervously replied.

'Lead the way to your vehicle.'

I just didn't like the look of him, and for some unknown reason I sensed he felt the same about me.

After explaining what he wanted me to do, he said in a very unfriendly manner, 'Move off when you are ready.'

My hands were shaking and I could feel the beads of perspiration running slowly down my brow. Many of the tasks that he asked me do, I had done on many occasions, but each one had to be performed to a very high standard with no allowances for any errors.

Halfway through, I already knew that I had blown it by not using the correct procedure for mutable roundabouts, along with not signalling at the right time. Then as we were returning to the test centre, the heavens opened. We weren't far from our destination when he instructed me to drive along Brooklands Road in Baguley, known for being full of potholes and drainage problems. As luck would have it, a lady was walking close to the edge of the kerb, as we were driving past her. There was no time to react as I ploughed into a massive trough of filthy water that churned upwards, towards and over her. She was caught in the entire onslaught of my mistake, and for a second or two she was entirely obscured by the wall of muck. The examiner's thunderous, red face and eviscerating glare told me all I needed to know. My chest tightened. I exhaled slowly, tried to lower tense shoulders, another long breath out. I knew then that I was doomed to fail, and I did. In the event, I failed on several counts.

I had to wait four weeks before I could retake the test, but my biggest concern was if I got him again. If I was unlucky to have him a second time, I knew that he would remember me from the Brocklands Road incident, which wouldn't be a good start for me. As it happened my luck was in and my examiner was the other guy. The test went really well for me and I felt confident and relaxed from start to finish. All my manoeuvres were perfect on our return back to the test centre, he just said in a nice, pleasant voice, 'I'm pleased to tell that you have passed.' Two down one to go, the final big test.

I had to work for a driving school as a trainee instructor to gain experience ready for the final part three. I would be self-employed, working under licence until qualified. This meant I had to pay for the hire of a car, plus the cost of the fuel and all other out-of-pocket expenses. The arrangement was that the company would provide the work. This was the only way that I could operate until I was confident enough to take the final exam. Once qualified, I would earn more and be able to establish my own business. After speaking with a few driving instructors at my local test centre, I was given contact details of a driving school in Urmston, Manchester.

Following a meeting and chat with the proprietor, he agreed to employ me as an unqualified trainee. His driving school provided me with a new, red Mini-Metro one up from the standard Mini. It was pretty standard for a learner's vehicle: easy on the controls with a tight turning circle but a rather inadequate gearbox. It was fitted with dual-controlled foot pedals, equipped with the company's livery and a detachable magnetic sign on the roof, which I could remove when it wasn't in use for lessons. Despite some shortcomings, it was a very economical car to run.

I had to sign a contract containing one particular clause specifying that if and when I passed the final part of the qualification, I had to remain with the school for a specified period. I think this was included so that drivers couldn't poach clients for their own future business. The fee that I paid to the company was around £175 per month. It is said that we never forget our first experience in whatever we do in life. This was true of the first lesson with my very first student.

She was a middle-aged, very poised, beautiful and sophisticated, not only in her manner, but in the way, she presented herself. She was about four foot nothing with high-heeled brown shiny shoes and sported round-framed, Harry Potter-style glasses. They seemed to rest more on her curved nose than on her ears. Radiating quiet refinement in her tartan skirt and tidy grey hair, she projected the air of an educated, potentially retired teacher every time she spoke. After having a friendly, preliminary chat with this lady and checking her driving licence details (which had to be done before allowing anybody to drive), we walked towards my car. I introduced myself as 'Alan'.

'What a nice name,' she twinkled, 'and I'm Catherine.' Leaning in, she whispered playfully into my ear.

'I bet if you turn around, you will see 'nosy Betty' next door peeping through her net curtains. She doesn't miss a trick, she probably thinks that you're my son or some young fancy-man who is taking me out for the day!' Her eyes sparkled.

'I think we'll keep her guessing, shall we?'

I smiled and replied, 'Yes, we will keep our secret.' From that moment on, I knew that this was a sweet lady with a sense of humour. She informed me that she had never had any lessons until this point. So, it was time to introduce her to the basic controls of the vehicle. I sat in the driver's seat, she in the front passenger seat. I went through all the controls whilst simultaneously reassuring her to encourage her confidence. What surprised me most was that she was very calm and focused on the job-in-hand.

It was standard practice to encourage a 'newbie' driver to practise driving skills in their local area, so that they would not be intimidated by unfamiliar surroundings. This was in order for her to familiarise herself with the controls and functions of the vehicle and the traffic conditions. At the same time, I reinforced my actions by giving her a running commentary of what I was doing and why. Eventually she ventured in a sweet and tentative voice,

'Can I have a go?'

I replied, 'My, you're keen, aren't you?'

I knew I would have my work cut out, this being her first time at the controls of a vehicle. I had discovered an unused piece of waste ground that used to be a department store. This would be an ideal place to let her loose in the driving seat. I brought the car to a stop in the car park. Glowing with excitement and anticipation she leapt from the passenger seat, scurrying over to the driver's seat. Her face was shining in the sunlight and I could see the child-like look of glee on her face. Before I could even exit the cramped driver's seat she ushered me to get out and let her 'take over'. However, whilst attempting to manoeuvre into the driver's side, her skirt unfortunately became tangled on the gear stick. To add to the chaos, she accidentally, and all a-fluster, caught her arm on the wiper controls. The wipers sprang into high-speed action, scraping horribly across the bone-dry windscreen and inevitably leaving unwelcome scratch lines on the glass.

After composing herself after this minor trauma, Catherine was able to sit in a normal driving position but because she was so small, the top of her head was almost in line with the upper part of the steering wheel. She tried to adjust the seat by following the instructions that I had given her. Things went from bad to worse. Whilst leaning forward and reaching for the seat adjustment lever directly under her seat, she hit her forehead on the steering wheel. Letting out a short cry of anger, she then tried again to make the adjustments. Finally, she adjusted the distance and the height to the desired position. I was already starting to feel exhausted and she had not even switched on the engine. There was still about twenty long minutes to go before the end of what was my gruelling debut lesson. Now Catherine was at the right height and raring to go - unlike me.

I tried to prolong the inevitable but she was eager to start the engine. She asked me for the keys and tried to insert one into the ignition but she had chosen the wrong one. I pointed meaningfully to the correct key but she seemed to panic and again slotted in the incorrect key. I asked her to pull the key back out whereupon she murmured sheepishly that she was trying to do that, but that it was stuck fast. I leaned over her knee to grab the jammed piece of metal that resembled a corkscrew. But it wouldn't budge. My horrified thought was disbelief at the unholy mess that had ensued from my very first student and a creeping dread at how I would explain this farce to my boss. I made my way around to the driver's side. As I tried to open her door, she became irritable.

'Look,' I growled, 'I'm trying to get us out of this mess before I have to notify my boss of the situation.'

She took one look at my angry face, then burst into tears. A woman was passing by. She strode grimly towards us.

'Everything alright?' she shouted.

I replied hastily, 'Yes, thanks we are just having a spot of bother trying to remove a jammed ignition key.'

'Oh dear, can I help? My husband is a mechanic, I only live around the corner.'

I coughed and mumbled, 'Thanks, but hopefully we should be okay!'

If I could just try and pull on it, get it yanked out. I leant over the now tearful learner who had been reduced to a sobbing, nervous wreck. After a tug-of-war with the now twisted key, I was able to re-insert it into the ignition. I reminded her of the observation checks before moving off. This was the moment she had been waiting for, and the moment I had been dreading...

I checked that all was clear. Now I had to instruct her to select first gear, at the same time depress the clutch and take the handbrake off. As any driver knows they all have to be applied in sync for a smooth drive from a parked position. This would be her first-ever lesson in control of a moving vehicle. I was starting to feel that my learner warranted an all-stations alert regarding an unexpected road hazard. It was now or never. My feet were trembling, but I had to cover the dual controls. The brake was my priority so my right foot hovered over the pedal. My next move was to assist her in releasing the handbrake. I reached over my seat to release the lever but she had got to it first. She tried to lower the handbrake without releasing the safety button at the end. She then simultaneously released the clutch and floored the accelerator. The car took an almighty lurch forward into the edge of the kerb. With the handbrake still engaged, the vehicle leapfrogged then stalled still stuck fast to the kerb. She still had her foot down hard on the accelerator, but there was no movement the car had jerked to a halt. Her response to this mayhem was to say, 'Have I done the right thing?'

Now I had to get us out of this mess. I asked her to just let go of the controls and try to get out of the driver's seat. She was in a state of mild shock, but she bravely insisted on carrying on with the driving. I glanced down at my left wrist to glimpse the time without her noticing me. This two-hour session seemed like an eternity.

There were still a few minutes of her lesson left. She shakily exited the driver's seat and with shaking knees returned to the helm. After straightening the car and extricating it from the now damaged kerb, I thought the best idea would be to remove ourselves from the 'scene of crime' in short order. I drove away as quickly as I could, but I knew that she would want to have another go before the end of the lesson. I had to conjure up a plan to put her off, if only for this lesson. I told her that we were low on fuel and would she mind if we went to fill up to which she reluctantly agreed. Great, I thought, this might be my chance to put her off the whole idea of driving! Nightmare scenarios ran through my fevered mind. What if she insisted on driving to the garage? She might smash into the petrol pumps and blow the garage and everybody in it to smithereens. Letting my learner loose would be like throwing a primed hand grenade into the forecourt.

I stealthily glimpsed at my watch - only a couple of minutes left, just enough time to pay for the fuel and take her home. On her next experience (if there were to be a second lesson), I decided that I would take her to a nearby car park to familiarise her with the controls. I just couldn't take the risk of her killing half of the residents of Sale. The start wasn't much better than the last time. But we did manage to engage the first gear then leapfrog our way forward.

I suggested that she just make a few figure-of-eight turns, but it became apparent that she could only steer the car to the left, but not to the right. With every attempt at crossing her arms to turn right, she got confused and this continued for the duration of the lesson.

The third lesson wasn't much better. On entering the car she manged to bang her head on the roof when getting into the passenger seat and let out a few Hail Marys before climbing in.

'Good morning,' I said.

'Morning, Sir, she muttered. 'Are we driving on the roads today, I'm keen to do so?'

My heart seemed to miss a few beats, before I could reply. 'Erm, yeah we could try later, but for now we will head for a quiet location just to recap and get you up and running again.

'Okay, I like that idea.'

Once we had parked up I swapped sides with her so now she was in the driver's seat and reluctantly raring to go, I quickly ran her through the controls to make sure that she could remember what we did on her first lesson.

'Are we ready to start the engine and slowly engage first gear?'

'Oh yes, can't wait. I was telling my next-door neighbour how much I was looking forward to venturing out on the roads.'

'Okay, let's give it a go then, when you are ready I would like you to move off very slowly keeping the car running in a straight line and under control if you can.'

To my surprise she seemed to have moved away reasonably steady. Now that we were moving I plucked up the courage to venture onto the road, while all the time being mindful of my dual controls and observations. I gently asked her to make a left turn when we got to the end of the short road. We were now driving using second gear. As we neared the short junction she began to gently push and pull the wheel round to the left while still in the same gear. When the short manoeuvre was almost complete, for no apparent reason she decided to turn the wheel the opposite way to the right. I quickly reached over, grabbed it and turned it back to the left in the direction of the road ahead. Then, without any hesitation, I used my controls to bring the car to a complete stop. She was now in a state of total confusion and seemed to be having a breakdown. After a short reprieve I asked her if she had just panicked or did she just make a mistake?

Her reply was, 'Well I was just doing a figure of eight like you taught me.' I drove her home, and unsurprisingly that was the last time that I saw her. Not sure if she continued or not, but not with me...

My next student was 'Julie', a charming young lady from Timperley, Cheshire, which was then a quaint sleepy village close to Altrincham. I knocked on her front door and was greeted by a lady who I assumed was her mum. We got chatting about her daughter who appeared from the rear kitchen.

'Hi.' I said, 'my name is Alan.'

She replied nervously, 'Hi Alan, I will be with you shortly, won't be a mo.'

'Okay,' I replied.

Julie joined me and disclosed that she had had many driving lessons with another driving school. My first impression was that she appeared to be very nervous and unsure of herself. I gave her the option of driving but she preferred that I drive a little further down the road.

Off we went to a nearby, quiet residential estate where Julie took over the driving. However, there was something bothering me about how she was holding the steering wheel. Her hands were in the right place, commonly known as the 'ten-to-two' position, but I noticed that both of her hands were shaking violently. I had never come across this before so it was quite disturbing. Because I had just met Julie for the first time, I didn't want to offend or distract her by continually looking at her hands. I therefore kept proceedings calm and business-like. 'When you feel comfortable, would you like to drive off when you are ready.'

'Okay, okay, I will...' she stuttered in reply.

After all necessary observations, she moved away quite smoothly. I was, however, very mindful of the heavy traffic and pedestrians who were near the kerbside. In this job, you have to have your wits about you all the time. Happily, she drove smoothly, and she was very alert. I think it was me who was the nervous one, especially with her fingers still flapping about with anxiety. Just as we were about to make a right turn at a busy junction, she hesitated before she committed to the manoeuvre so I had to make an immediate drive for the steering wheel to avoid a near-miss with an oncoming truck. Once we were clear of the danger, I asked her whether she was okay.

She replied with a stammer, 'Yeh, yeh, I think so...'

Then I noticed that her hands were shaking even more violently than before. I thought the best thing would be to pull over to let her compose herself before making our way back to her house. I did feel sorry for her, after what had otherwise been a good drive. As she walked up to her pathway, she hesitated, before turning around to give me a wave and I later wrote some notes about her lack of what appeared to be self-control.

Julie surprised me as we started her second lesson a week later. She disclosed that she suffered from a nervous disorder, but that she had not wanted to raise this during her first lesson in case I didn't want to teach her to drive. My response was to assure her that it wasn't a problem, and now that I was aware of her issues, we could overcome them. The simple act of disclosure seemed to do the trick as she became more confident, not only with her driving but in her self-belief about her ability to overcome her nervousness. She did eventually pass her driving test on the first attempt.

Next was a young woman from Sale in Cheshire who resided in one hell of a house that was more like a mansion in its scale. Upon arrival, I noticed that the vast driveway had ample parking space for about eight cars or more. As I sprayed some small amounts of gravel while coming to a halt beside the other high-end cars, my little Mini Metro suddenly seemed a bit incongruous. I counted at least five, if not six luxury vehicles, one a Rolls Royce, another a vintage Jaguar, identified by its old registration plate. This latter car really stood out from the crowd. It was snowy white with a bright silver trim along the doors and sleek whitewall tyres. Its headlights seemed to have eyes running in the centre of the glass lens. I got the strangest feeling that the massive, glassy orbs were watching me, almost mocking me. It seemed like quite a trek to the enormous wooden door fronted by a sweep of marble steps. Before I could ring the doorbell, the colossal mahogany door swung open, and there stood my new learner, dressed in a bright green school uniform, gold trims around the edges of her jacket. She looked about fifteen but had to be seventeen or more because that was the criteria for a provincial driving licence. She spoke with a well-educated voice.

'Hi,' she whispered, 'I'm Elanor.'

'Hello, Elanor, my name is Alan. I will be taking over from your usual instructor.'

'Okay, pleased to meet you, Alan.'

'No problem.'

Elanor was confident enough to take the wheel right away and drove like somebody with substantial experience. The hour seemed to pass very quickly before we headed back to her house. She was charming throughout the short drive. It wasn't too long after a few more lessons with her I suggested that she applied for her driving test.

'Wow,' she echoed. 'Am I really ready for my test?'

I replied, 'Yes you will be by the time your appointment comes around.'

'Okay, she said I will apply today.'

After only a couple more lessons she took the test and passed with flying colours. The delight as her lovely blue eyes lit up like firecrackers. It was difficult not knowing what to expect from each of my learners without judging them on their first impressions. I hadn't built up enough of a client base of students in the early stages of my career. The company that I worked for insisted that when I became a fully qualified instructor, I should sign a contract. I guess the reason for this was so that I wouldn't start working for myself and start my own driving school. However, unbeknownst to them, I had applied for my final exam and was allocated a date. Again, the test centre was in Sale, Cheshire, which was good news for me because I was familiar with the area.

I was being examined as a professional driver, not a learner, but I had to be careful not to be spotted by any other driving instructor from the same school. I sat nervously in the waiting room and just like my students, felt like an executioner was about to appear from the bowels of the dimly lit room with its door ajar. The waiting seemed to last an eternity, so much was at stake, and I knew that I had to pull this off. I didn't want to go through this torture ever again. A man appeared from the room and gently called out my name in a soft, friendly, southern accent which immediately made me relax. As luck would have it, he was the examiner I had had for my part two retest, which I passed with flying colours. No Mr Nasty this time.

As we made our way to the parked car, I tried to pull the keys from my side pocket but they got caught up. The more I tugged at them, the more tangled they became. Eventually, they became free. I couldn't say the same for my nerves. I was a wreck. At this point, I could hardly speak. Considering that I was always telling my students to relax and stay calm before a test, I was now in their shoes. The first half of the test involved me 'acting' as instructor to the examiner who played the 'learner' with around four driving lessons under his belt. This would include me instructing him on the driving manoeuvres that a novice would be shown, and not to overestimate his experiences. I had to treat him like any other student, chatting with him about his previous driving lessons and whether there was any specific driving 'issues' he wanted to address.

He replied, 'Yes, I have problems with the signalling when approaching roundabouts.'

I replied, 'What don't you understand about them?'

'I'm not sure of the system when approaching the lanes and what signal to use before entering any junctions.'

At this point, I had to be thinking ahead of my game. This is where I could be caught out. I needed to take in all the information that the examiner was telling me. If I assessed him as having too much or too little knowledge, I risked failure. It was crucial that I give no other instructions other than dealing with roundabouts. I decided to show him images from the highway code, knowing full well that he would have seen this information when he was learning about the rules of the road. I thought that if I could somehow use up some of the hour-long lesson using this method, then it would shorten the test, but at the same time delay the inevitable pressure I would be under whilst giving him further instructions when we were out on the road. Once he had confirmed that he now had a better understanding, I asked him if he would like to put into practice what we had just discussed.

To my relief he replied, 'No, I'm now more than happy with what you have explained to me. I now feel more confident in dealing with roundabouts.'

Afterwards he made a few notes, but I knew that there was more to come and that I wasn't going to be off the hook that easily. After a short silence, he informed me that he had an issue with hill-starts. Luckily, this was an excellent manoeuvre for me to teach because I had experience with other students who found this challenging. This time I didn't refer to the highway code but we did have a general chat about how to approach the inclines and gradients of various hills, using the handbrake and the right amount of 'biting point' acceleration, synchronising the clutch, handbrake and accelerator. At this point, he told me that his previous instructor had never taught him this method. I took this opportunity to take control of the lesson and informed him that maybe it would be a good idea to drive to a nearby area where there was a fairly steep hill where I would get him to practice.

Halfway up the hill, I asked him to pull over safely, select neutral and apply the handbrake. He brought the car into a stop alongside the kerb.

'When you are ready,' I intoned in my best, 'calm instructor' mode, 'I would like you to pull away from the kerbside after using your observations and in a controlled manner.'

My experienced instructor made a good first attempt at jerking up the hill like a beginner so I suggested that he stop the car and pretend to settle down a little, then try again. This time he made a perfect hill-start under full control.

Both of us were effectively play acting. He was actually pretending to drive less skilfully than he actually could, just like a learner. If I didn't have to take him seriously just to get through the test his performance was hilarious but very professional.

'Please continue and follow the road ahead.'

He acknowledged my request and continued. Once we were away from the busy road, I asked him how he now felt about dealing with hill-starts.

He replied by saying that he now felt a lot more confident and relaxed and I didn't have to give him any more directions for returning back to the test centre but I was still in control of the lesson until we arrived back I knew we were not far from the base but couldn't afford to be complacent despite having a good feeling about the outcome of the test. Sure enough, he sprang his last trap when making a right turn from a busy road into a side road. His driving and indicating procedures were correct but once we had completed the turn and after waiting for a truck pass, he asked whether he should have waited (as he had done before making the manoeuvre), or just turned?

I replied, 'No, you had done the right thing to wait. Oncoming vehicles should not have to slow down or stop if they have right of way.' He smiled reassuringly. I know that the wrong advice from me would have certainly cost me the test, even at the eleventh hour. When we arrived back at the centre, he switched the engine off and politely handed me the keys. All he said before walking off was, 'You will hear from us very soon!'

As dawn broke the next day I was still anxiously awake and heard the faint swish and click of post dropping on the hall floor. Although not expecting my DVLA result so soon, I could not help scurrying downstairs with a painfully beating heart. I spotted the buff envelope under the pile, snatched it up, dropped it from my trembling hands, retrieved it and then spotted the DVLA stamp. Time seemed to stop. My life was about to change again (or not!) in the murky dawn of my hallway and it all centred on a dreary brown envelope. Fumbling with the contents, I glimpsed the first few words and knew all was well. I had done it. I was now a fully qualified Approved Driving Instructor. I stood, rooted to the spot and in a daze. Then my wife walked up to me, and said,

'Is there something wrong?'

'No, no, there isn't.'

'Well what then, why are you looking at that letter as though there is a problem?'

'I can't believe it.'

'What can't you believe?' she asked impatiently.

'This letter, it says I passed my final test yesterday.'

'Oh my god, does that mean that you can now teach on your own?'

'Erm yeah, it does.'

'Wow, you did it, I'm so proud of you, I really am!'

I must have read the letter about fifty times before it started to sink in. Later on, I received a phone call from my employer's daughter, who worked for him in the office. What came next took me completely by surprise. She congratulated me on my test result, which took me aback. I hesitated before asking,

'What do you mean?'

'You took your part three test yesterday, didn't you?'

I didn't reply straight away.

'Alan, are you still there?' she asked.

'Yes, I'm still here, how did you know that?'

'One of our instructors saw you yesterday at Sale Test Centre with the examiner in your car, she said that you looked happy.'

She then went on to ask why I hadn't informed her about what I was doing, and that she had learnt that I might have passed the final test. Then she made a sarcastic comment about 'going behind their backs' and asked icily, 'Did you intend not to tell us?'

I indignantly replied, 'I didn't know that you were keeping tabs on me.'

'No, we're not, but it would have been a gesture of protocol to inform us of your intentions.'

'Well, anyway, how did you know that I passed?'

'We have our sources,' she remarked enigmatically, '...so, will you be coming in soon to sign a contract as part of the agreement when you started with us?'

Well, of course, I will be continuing with my lessons tomorrow morning.'

'Can you at some point pop in to see me, I will have your contract ready for signing?'

'Yeah, yes, I suppose so.'

I had no intention of signing any Micky Mouse contract with them or any another school. From then, I just avoided going into their office, even though she kept on insisting that I sign. A few weeks later I left them and went to work for the British School of Motoring in the city centre. I now had more experience and was working for a very reputable company. Many of the learners were from diverse backgrounds such as university students –not what I was used to. On my first day I was allocated a young lad, who at first seemed to know everything about nothing. He was a gangling skinny kid with rings sticking out of his ears and nose; a face full of metal that chinked at every movement. Once inside the car I asked him for his licence.

'Not gorrit,' he gasped with his smelly breath. Cannabis. I could smell it anywhere on anybody. I had never forgotten the pungent smell of dope, from my seafaring time on the South African coast. I turned to him sternly.

'I need to see it to confirm that it's up-to-date.'

'I just said mate that I ain't gorrit.'

'Well in that case we can't proceed with the lesson.'

'What ya mean mate, "can't have my lesson"?'

'Without sight of the licence we can't go any further.'

'Fuck this... I've fucking paid for ten lessons, my old man will fucking kill me.'

'No need for that language either.'

'I'm gonna complain.'

'That's up to you, but they will only say the same as I have done.'

He stormed out of the vehicle after I aborted the lesson, but oddly enough bypassed the driving school and failed to play holy hell as I'd expected. I certainly did not want any more, cocky gobshite 'clients' like him! Happily, I never heard any more about the incident.

My next learner was another, much more sensible lad. He had had a very negative experience with his last instructor. They had nearly come to blows but he was a bit reluctant to discuss it. But after a short drive he told me that his instructor was very aggressive towards him because he was gay. He seemed happier with me and continued with his lessons until he passed his test then thanked me for supporting him, while others wouldn't.

Next in the car was a young Indian lady who could barely speak a word of English so I had my work cut out trying to communicate and mainly used sign language rather than speaking. She was a very sweet lady, but the language issue was fairly insurmountable. On one occasion, I asked her to follow the road ahead and she continued to drive without observing the road signs. I knew that at the next junction the road became a bus lane. I was becoming anxious as to what she was intending to do at the lights. I tried to give her some verbal instructions, to no avail. Close to the junction, it was obvious that she was going to enter the bus lane. I had no choice but to take over the steering wheel, haul it round to the right, and change gear using the dual controls, to avoid a catastrophe. She did continue with her lessons, but after a while she became pregnant and told me she would stop having lessons for now, and restart after her baby was born.

After three years of driving instruction, I was starting to flag. I had lost count of how many near misses I'd had, and to grab the steering wheel at the same time as hitting the dual-controlled pedals. Negotiating the highways and byways of Britain's cluttered, congested, potholed and often gridlocked road systems tested my nerves, and some of the students stretched them to breaking point. Hundreds of students had sweaty hands and had clutched the wheel and ground the gears of my little Metro in the three years of my teaching. It was a job that certainly gave me experience of people in all their glory and how they react under pressure: the talkers, the defensive and anxious ones, the braggarts, the meek mice who turned into raging furies behind the wheel. I saw it all and learnt how to stifle my own fear and impatience, presenting a calm and reassuring face to the world…

I had endured anxiety attacks, almost had a nervous breakdown and lost count of how many times I had caught the flu bug from all the coughing, sneezing, and filthy hands in the cockpit and at the controls of the cars that had been allocated to me. I had also gained a substantial amount of weight and my hair began to thin. How anybody could survive a lifetime in the world of newbie learner drivers was beyond me but I knew it was high time to change jobs.

CHAPTER SIX

CAPTAIN CARGO – THE FRANCHISE

After I finished with my driving instructor career in 1989, I knew that I wanted to remain self-employed. I had some redundancy savings left but had to use them wisely, not squander them on some lame duck business or new venture. I had a family to support and a mortgage to pay after all. My son Paul and I went to check out a franchise exhibition taking place at the Manchester GMEX centre. I knew that there would be a variety of exhibitors there throughout the week. The last time that I walked into this magnificent building was when I caught a train from there on my way to join a ship in Liverpool many years before.

The building used to be Manchester's Central Railway Station but is currently the site of the Nightingale Covid-19 hospital (more about that later). It was a freezing winter morning as we entered the glass doors of the centre, and after paying a couple of quid entrance fee, security gave us ID badges. All the major players were offering franchise packages, and putting on a show in the hope that they could sell their companies and help them to expand their business.

Central station (later GMEX) in its heyday

We decided to make a day of it and have some lunch from the centre's canteen. Halfway through the day, we were already becoming bored with the relentless sales pitching from the promoters and there wasn't much that appealed to me. The ones that did were well beyond my budget of around £10,000. We then spotted a stall that stood out with its colourful displays. It was the 'Captain Cargo' logo that caught my eye. I was expecting some gimmick, such as a franchise for a window cleaning business, or something bizarre and funny. It was actually a franchise for a freight company offering to sell a post-coded area to set up a courier business. They offered to train would-be investors to manage their operation working alongside the parent company with all the start-up vehicle livery, and all the support and back-up that was needed to launch the franchise and build it into a successful business.

After thinking it over I revisited the venue to make further enquiries with the Captain Cargo franchise. The initial set-up fees were around £10,000, which included the first monthly vehicle rental, along with all the livery and franchise package. I had a solicitor check the contract to ensure that I wasn't getting ripped off. After getting the all-clear, I paid the full fee, which granted me the right to operate for five years under license. If by then my business was up and running, there was a renewal option for a further five years without any additional costs. We were operating out of Manchester Airport; a central point with easy access to the motorway network, and utilising an existing freight company because it was a new enterprise with only limited franchises.

My franchised areas were SK1 to SK6: Stockport/Cheshire postcodes. Our uniforms had the Captain Cargo logo emblazoned prominently on the front that made it feel embarrassingly like a Superhero outfit. The livery was also displayed all around my VW Luton box van.

It was time to get out on the road with the salesman who had been allocated to me as part of the training package. I had paid for a business that was originally part of an overnight parcel delivery company that already had an established customer base. The franchise fees were charged according to how much revenue the company had generated as a going concern. However, the training was a joke. The professed 'salesman', who was supposed have been in the parcel delivery business, had never done this kind of work before and knew as much about sales as I did about flying a 747. Nonetheless, as each day went by I grew in confidence at finding my way around and introducing myself to the customers, but inevitably had a few bumps and scrapes with the unfamiliar vehicle.

One day I noticed another Captain Cargo van picking up parcels within my designated area. Apparently, it was a 'house account' which was one that was owned and run by the franchisor giving them the right to encroach on any designed area as long as it was written into my franchise holder's agreement. This had not been done in my case so the company was technically in breach of contract. I challenged management who insisted it was house accounts and they were entitled to operate wherever they chose. I wasn't happy with this and noted that my franchise agreement did not stipulate that the company could collect parcels within a franchised area and keep the revenue for themselves. I warned them that I would take my franchise agreement to my solicitor, emphasising that I wasn't happy that the company had decided to work within my area without my knowledge or prior permission.

After examining the agreement my solicitor confirmed that there was nothing to say, that the company had the right to work within my area without my permission. Legally, there was no such thing as a house account. His advice was to inform my manager that as per legal advice the company was acting unfairly and to give them forty-eight hours to cease and desist from collecting from these two accounts, before handing them over to me. A few days later, the manager's response was that these two accounts were too big for me to handle on a daily basis. It felt like a stand-off, especially as they continued with their spurious house account actions regarding collections. The revenue from the parcels I was collecting each day didn't really amount to much, but having those two, additional big accounts would make my own business a lot more lucrative. I had no choice but to instruct my solicitor to contact them and make the position clear.

Within a day the company salesman was on the phone being conciliatory and pleading with me to leave things as they were as I would 'not be able to cope' with the weight of all the additional parcels. I indignantly assured him I could indeed 'cope' and that I would be taking over the accounts from the following Monday morning. I also advised him to cease sending his vehicle within my franchised postcodes. The line went quiet for a moment, then he said ambiguously, 'Okay - but you might regret this.'

They had obviously realised that I wasn't bluffing and that they had to hand over these two substantial accounts, but I have always believed in standing up for your rights. Nonetheless, I did realise that maybe this would make me very unpopular with the company. Still, my emotions were at an all-time high, I felt quite pleased with myself for challenging the management, and emerging as the winner. An abrupt phone call from the manager informed me that I would be taking over the two so-called house accounts from the following Monday. My biggest concern was whether I could indeed fit all the heavy freight and parcels onto my van without breaking the law by it being overweight. It was starting to dawn on me that I was now on my own and (for obvious reasons) couldn't ask for help. I only had the one van and had no contingency plans so if I came unstuck, I no-one to call upon for help.

Monday morning arrived and after finishing my morning deliveries, I decided to make a courtesy call to my new customers, introduce myself, and get an estimate of their daily output. This was a wise move because once I got to know the dispatchers I was able to make arrangements with them to call me and give me some warning during the day of what they would be dispatching. This enabled me to call in and collect some of the parcel load earlier before heading to base at Manchester airport.

In time, I was in the position of having spare funds available to invest in future projects. I wanted to expand but there were no more postcodes available that would link to my existing area. I then heard about a franchisee selling up his business. The only downside was that it covered the other side of Manchester to mine, including Salford, Radcliffe and Bury. The business was for sale at £30,000. On its own it was hard to tell whether this was a realistic figure but my determination to acquire the franchise was boosted once I realised that other people were also showing an interest. This also acted against me during negotiations as it meant the seller would not negotiate due to other interested parties. I had to get another bank loan which was granted due to my success with the original franchise.

The new franchise would involve hiring additional vehicles and two more drivers. I was apprehensive about working an area that didn't link with my existing franchise but my entrepreneurial spirit got the better of me, and I went ahead and signed the additional franchise contracts which would take effect almost immediately. There wasn't much existing business and customer base in the areas, but with my newly acquired sales experience I was able to build upon the existing business opportunities and also familiarise myself with the new postcode areas involved.

Three months later the cracks started to appear as I tried to run two disparate businesses. There were all sorts of logistical issues in working both sides of Manchester and Stockport. The pressure started to take its toll on my finances, and my health and wellbeing. Even worse, word was reaching management that I was gaining a reputation for not running the business properly, and in line with my contract's terms and conditions. This gave them the opportunity to use payback tactics, and I was called into the office on many occasions. They asked why I wasn't fulfilling my franchise obligations. This worried me because I knew that I could not expect any support from the managers, even though they were supporting others in similar circumstances. It was obviously a golden opportunity for them to disrupt my running of the business so that they could build a case against me for when the contracts came up for renewal. The contracts ran for a five-year term with the proviso that the business was built up and duties satisfactorily undertaken (including all financial matters and bookkeeping) contracts would automatically run for another five years without any fees paid.

Just to exacerbate the situation, I started having staff problems including one employee who either turned up late or failed to come in at all. Each morning I would arrive at work before my drivers to ensure that their deliveries were available, and verify that they would be arriving on time to start their day's work. Mobile phones back then were not as common as now but I allowed each driver to take theirs home with them. One individual had no intention of coming into work and kept his phone switched off. He called the office later in the day and gave them a lame duck excuses of a flat battery. To make matters worse the office worker 'Cath' (not her real name) inexplicably took this opportunity to consistently score points with management with her accusations that I was failing to run the business properly. This constant negativity was intimidating to me and the drivers.

My marriage had also started to show some cracks. I had not been happy for some time. My younger sister Linda lived in North Wales and she had always been there for me so at weekends, I would go and stay with her. She lived in a very quiet secluded area that had one shop, a post office and a nice country pub just across the road. In the evening, I would walk over to the Trefnent Inn for a couple of beers just to chill out. The landlady, Sue (Sue), was young and very cheerful and over the course of a few weekend visits to Wales, I began a friendship with her. However, Sue's parents and brother all lived in the pub. It was a family concern with the father financing the running of the business. It wasn't too long before we became partners but she was 20 years younger than me and I was still married. At weekends I would stay at the pub till closing time, then when her parents had gone upstairs to sleep, we would go to the nightclubs in Rhyl. This blossoming relationship didn't go down too well with Sue's parents, especially her father who was very strict. Her mum, Pauline, however, was charming and easy-going. After a while I became really friendly with Sue's mum, but not so much her dad. It was noted by the family and my sister Linda that this relationship with Sue was becoming serious. It was an increasing wrench to travel back and forth to Manchester to run my business from Monday to Friday.

The new franchise area that I had bought seemed to be (slowly but surely) becoming more profitable. My daughter Rachel was now fending for herself and courting Rod, a personable young man. In July 1997 she became pregnant and everyone was delighted, not least me, as this would be my first grandchild. The pregnancy proceeded normally and she had a baby boy called Cameron. We were all over the moon but this blessedness was shattered when I received a heart-breaking call from her two days later to say that the baby had developed sepsis and died. Rachel and Rod were distraught as were her mother and I. It seemed inconceivably cruel that this could happen to her after carrying the baby for nine months. I visited Rachel in Wythenshawe Hospital and it took just one look to see her crushing hurt at the loss of her first child. It was very hard for me to hold back the tears.

My other immediate family concern was my son Paul who needed a job. I worried about him. I knew he had some issues not with his mother Deirdre, but with some bullying boys in the area and this bothered me a lot. One evening while I was in the pub having a beer with Sue, my wife Deirdre phoned me. She was so upset I could hardly understand what she was trying to tell me. After I calmed her down she told me that Paul and his friends had been attacked whilst out. The line went quiet for some time while the seriousness of the situation sank in. I asked Deirdre how bad Paul's injuries were.

She managed to tell me there were some cuts and bruises but the situation was not helped by my own sense of guilt regarding the mental wellbeing of my children together with the fact that my wife was shouldering the burden of parenting with no husband to support her. I went to see him and Rachel as much as I could, whilst reassuring them both that I was always there and I would always be there for them. However, Deirdre sensed my guilt so exaggerated the crisis which I suspected was a tactic to get me to return to her at home in Wythenshawe. Paul was now old enough to have driving lessons and I knew he wanted a car. He soon passed his test and this is where I came in. I helped him to get his first car (a Ford I think) but it wasn't too long before he had a few 'bumps'. So, Bank of Dad came to the rescue and helped him to get a white BMW with all the trimmings and extras - just what a young lad dreams of. Giving Paul some practical support helped mitigate some of the guilt I was feeling for not being there for him and my daughter Rachel during this challenging time.

Eventually I was able to get Paul to work with me at the delivery franchise, now that he had a full driving license. It wasn't too long before I was able to leave him on his own because he seemed to pick the job up fairly quickly. It worked much better for me to have somebody that I could trust and to leave him to it. However, it inevitably caused some issues with the office staff and eventually the management because they felt he was getting the job was because he was my son.

My wife eventually suspected that I was seeing someone, and it was very difficult for me to lie my way out of this dilemma. Sue and I would see as much of each other as we could but she also had a business to run. I knew that her father, Brian, did not approve of me seeing his younger daughter and he didn't even know that I was still married! It was a very difficult time for both of us. I suggested to Sue that she discuss the situation with her dad and to just tell him that I was divorced. She thought that was a good idea and went along it. I know that she had a long discussion with Brian and told him that she would like me to move in with her on a permanent basis. It wasn't long before I moved in with Sue in her room at the pub.

I knew deep down Brian didn't approve. He would make it obvious and went out of his way to make me feel uncomfortable whenever he could. When I arrived at the pub in the evening, I would go straight up to the living quarters with my bag before going down to the bar to greet Sue. He would close their lounge door so that I wouldn't enter the room and watch the TV. There were times when he would be drinking in the bar with his mates but never invited me to join them.

Sue's brother Gary seemed to be very jealous of our relationship and would also go out of his way to score points with his dad. If there were chores that hadn't been done around the pub at weekends when I was there, like cleaning the beer cellar, he would grass on us to his father hoping that it would cause trouble between Sue and her dad. The kitchen wasn't very big, so it was difficult for me to navigate my way around the family while they were all sitting at the table. Brian and Gary would make it awkward for me to get in and eat. I got the impression that they thought, or were hoping, I would go away one day and wouldn't be part of Sue's life anymore. That didn't happen as we became more and more fond of each other. Some weekends if a member of her staff phoned in sick, she would ask me help out behind the bar and pull pints for the customers, something that I hadn't done before, but at the same time I got to enjoy it and the banter with the customers, some who would try and tease Sue about our age difference. Being the only pub in the village, everybody knew everybody's business and there were always some who would get pleasure out of exaggerating and spreading gossip.

After little training, I enjoyed my unpaid, part-time job. I soon made many friends who would come for a drink and join me in the friendly atmosphere of the pub. Customers and family members began to accept me for who and what I was. Even Sue's aunties and uncles would occasionally visit for Sunday lunch and family gatherings after closing time. Lighting the coal fire in the lounge became one of my chores so it wasn't too long before one of Sue's aunties nicknamed me the 'Stoker.' I seemed to be accepted more as time went by despite Brian's ongoing hostility. Nevertheless, I was happy where I was, and a lot happier in this environment than in my home life. I missed my children and my wife who was a good woman and a fantastic mother for whom I had a lot of respect. However, as time went by my love for her was receding. I would always ensure that she was not short of anything.

In 1997, Sue received some bad news from my elder brother Arthur in New Zealand. His youngest son, my nephew Tommy, who was only nineteen years old, had had an accident while out with his mates. This was very disturbing and upsetting news. Eventually, I got the dreaded phone call from my brother informing me that Tommy had passed away in hospital. I was devastated; no parent wants to see their child die. Arthur and I were very close, more like mates. Young Tommy was a strong good-looking young man who lived life to the full. He often went down to the local beach to surf with his mates so it was such a terrible loss of life at an early age. My brother and Diane, his wife, were heartbroken.

I had to make a quick decision whether to drop everything and go to New Zealand or stay at home and keep in contact with my brother. I knew Arthur needed some family support but I was in a very difficult position with my job, and there was nobody to look after my business if I was away. The flight to Auckland New Zealand would take about thirty-six hours, plus the onward flight to New Plymouth where my brother lived. Due to purchasing the second franchise, I was very short of funds but I decided that I had no option but to fly out to New Zealand. Sue booked my tickets to New Zealand for the next day. This involved a flight to London, another to Singapore for a stopover of a few hours, then from there to Auckland, New Zealand. Finally, the domestic flight to my brother's hometown of New Plymouth, North Island. At the check-in desk at Heathrow an airline representative asked me if I was off to Kiwi for a holiday. When I told her of my family loss, I could tell that she felt uncomfortable and regretted asking. She said sympathetically 'Oh

I'm really sorry, how awful, what a terrible and tragic time this must be for you all.'

She arranged for priority tags to be put on all my luggage to save time in New Zealand which was a thoughtful gesture. On arrival in Auckland my baggage was the first to appear on the carousel (I kept those labels on throughout my journey and on the return flights home). I was worn out and had been travelling for around three days without much sleep, apart from the cat-naps on the flight. As regards to the franchise business, I didn't really have much contact and had to rely on Paul relaying developments to my wife who kept me in touch.

I was greeted at the airport in New Plymouth by my brother Arthur. Superficially, he seemed okay but I knew he was just putting on a front for my sake. We drove to his house where I met his wife Diane and their daughters Robina and Claudine. As expected they were heartbroken but I was welcomed with open arms, and the tears began to flow. I knew that it was a very sad emotional time for all, yet nobody appeared to want to talk about the sad events. I think that everybody was in a state of shock and despair. Arthur and I had a few beers then he opened up and told me what had happened to Tommy and about the funeral arrangements. Tommy would be cremated. Tommy rested overnight in his home at Bell Block, New Plymouth where he was raised, then as per his mother's Maori culture, onto the Owae Marae (meeting house) in Waitara, Taranaki for two nights.

Because his family appreciated it would be a big funeral, they knew the Marae would hold a lot of people even though a lot of folks still had to stand outside. Cremation is generally not part of the Maori culture, hence why there wasn't many family members who were deeply entrenched in this tradition attended the cremation and some who weren't Maori.

Top left Paul (my son) Top right Graham (Linda's son) middle left Tommy (Arthur and Diane's son) middle right Jenny (Mike and Jean's daughter). The one down on the right, Claire. (Mike and Jean's daughter. Bottom right Mike (Michael and Jean's son) Bottom left Emma (Susan and Stephen's daughter).

On the day of the funeral there was a huge gathering of Tommy's friends, who came with surfboards as a sign of respect. After the ceremonies one of Arthur's close friends invited me to go for a beer with him in downtown New Plymouth, just to give everybody some time to comfort each other. After a couple of days, it was apparent that there was nothing more that I could do or say to my brother and his family. So, it was time to return back home to the UK and back to my work.

The journey home was very subdued and I wasn't looking forward to whatever was awaiting me when I got back. I knew that if there had been problems there would have been no one to help and no chance of assistance from the management or my fellow franchisees. Sue was at the airport to take me home. We didn't really say much to each other on the journey home where I showered and collapsed into bed. Before I could sleep, Sue came in to say that my son Paul had phoned her as he had broken down in Salford. I was so tired I couldn't even think straight. Paul told me the vehicle would not start and he was only halfway through a day's work. We lived quite a distance from Salford but true to form, the depot manager was uncooperative when I phoned him, saying he could do nothing and it was my responsibility to get the parcels from Paul's van delivered safely. These were the people that were supposed to be supporting me but never did. I knew that Sue was upset for me and was reluctant for me to go out, insisting that the company needed to resolve the problem. But I knew different. I was on my own so had no choice but to drive to Salford in the spare van, reeling with tiredness and jet lag in order to rescue Paul and get the deliveries done.

I was feeling very resentful. The management were all aware where I had been and why, yet they didn't care. I had been a marked man from the day I demanded my first two customers back and threatened litigation. This was payback but it still angered me that they could be so callous, knowing full well that I had just returned from the funeral of my nephew.

The following morning, I went to the depot to make sure the lads were okay. The manager informed us both that Paul's outstanding items had to be delivered before 10am before he could start on the day's work. The day went sharply downhill from there. Paul told me there was no way he could do it. I was still very jet lagged and confronted the manager. To be frank, I gave him a 'bollocking' and didn't let him get word in. I could have punched him for not supporting me in the dire situation I was in. He didn't care less.

One my other drivers then informed me that he had broken the tachograph (that records the speed of the vehicle when it is in motion – a legal requirement) on his 7½ ton, brand new truck. It had to be taken off the road, and consequently cost me £350 to repair. I later learned that the driver didn't lock the tachograph cover which was designed to prevent it from opening. It was as though everybody thought that I had just swanned off to New Zealand for a holiday and that I had left them all in the lurch to just get on with it. Nothing could have been further from the truth. I had no regrets about going to New Zealand to support my brother and his family but the overall experience had left me financially and emotionally drained. However, I had no choice but to just get on with picking up the pieces and to move on.

My relationship with backstabbing office worker Cath had deteriorated over time. Her machinations had included befriending my other drivers to get them to turn against me and make life difficult for me. My sporadic attempts to patch things up met with a brick wall response so I was making enemies I could have done without. Rumours started to circulate about cracks appearing within the company and that we were losing a lot of customers who were taking their business elsewhere. This disturbed me because I had built this business up almost from scratch. The only way I could discover the truth was to visit the customers that I had lost. After calling on several of my clients, I was informed that my company was making a mess of their accounts and overcharging them for the wrong service. This was profoundly affecting my business and revenue. Further investigation revealed that this was happening nationwide with all our other customers. We formed an action group after some franchisee meetings and our nominated rep approached management with our findings. Predictably they denied that any problems existed and that we were doing really well. However, soon my monthly pay cheque showed discrepancies between my invoiced figures and what should have been credited to my account. This was explained as just 'an accounting error' that would be rectified the following month. It never happened, so my monthly income was dwindling. Our depot manager echoed the company line saying that everything was okay. It was 'just a few mistakes' that would be put right. The writing was well and truly on the wall as far as my business and franchise were concerned.

It was a critical situation as my vehicles were on hire and lease. The Mercedes-Benz truck and Sprinter van, were on a four-year fixed lease, which left three years left to pay on both. With a dwindling income and customer base, I also had to pay mobile phone bills, staff and accountant's bills as well as keeping tax returns completed and up to date. I now had to plan ahead and be ready for the worst, which was looming. I started laying off a couple of my drivers.

I was only using one vehicle for the two franchises, down from four. I was the only one left covering what remained of the ashes of a once thriving business. Towards the end I wasn't receiving any payments at all from the company. I wrote letters to my debtors asking for more time to make the monthly payments. They agreed to this for a short while, but before long I realised I had no revenue at all to keep up my monthly payment plan because my franchise business had collapsed.

Luckily Paul had already left to start a new job. Not long after this I was only using one vehicle for the two franchises, down from four. While things were still buoyant, I had managed to scrape some money together for a deposit and a mortgage on a brand new, four-bedroom house in Runcorn, Cheshire, with Sue. I set myself up as a same-day courier working from home as a base, using the Sprinter van which was ideal for this kind of work. The first thing was to visit factories at the nearby industrial estate and distribute flyers with my contact details. The next day I got my lifeline via a phone call from a manager at one of the factories that dealt in food distribution on a massive scale. He asked whether I was available to call round and deliver some food to a care home. I was up bright and early the next morning, smartly dressed with a gleaming vehicle. I was led into a warehouse and given some food items to deliver to a care home within the Liverpool area. The job was done and I confirmed this with

Bob, the manager, who then asked me to make several deliveries to various destinations in the Lake District. As the weeks passed I was at his premises on a daily basis so I felt as though I had landed on my feet. I became well acquainted with the manager and staff who were pleased with my service. My fees were promptly paid by their accounts department so I didn't really need to look elsewhere for work. At last I was able to pay off some of my debts and keep up with the monthly mortgage payments of our new home.

When my divorce was finally absolute, I asked Sue to marry me. She didn't hesitate to say 'yes', because she had already dropped many hints. I knew this wouldn't go down too well with her father but to my surprise he seemed to accept me and was happy for Sue. Brian and Pauline were determined to spare no expense for their daughter's wedding. It took place nearby in a quaint little village near to where we lived in Darsbury. The reception was held at the magnificent Crewe Hall in Cheshire, a Jacobean manor house that was once part of the Queen's estate. The day of the wedding was on the same date as her father's birthday 29th of December 2000.

There were many family issues to resolve. Apart from Brian having reservations about the wedding, I was never asked about my brothers and sisters. Sue's family were aware that my mother was alive and that she wasn't very well, but other than that we never seemed to talk about families, apart from occasionally my children Rachel and Paul. I therefore had to decide who was to represent my side of the family. Sue's parents had only met my sister Linda and her family from my side. I was very close to Linda because she had supported me throughout all the difficulties I was facing. So, I decided that she would attend the wedding ceremony as the representative of my side of the family. The invitations were duly sent out, including some to my nearby family, but Sue suggested that I invite Arthur over from New Zealand to be my best man. I wasn't sure if it was either fair or a good idea to ask him to travel such a long distance Nevertheless, I invited my brother over along with his current girlfriend (he had divorced his wife Diane) they arrived just a few days before the wedding and stayed with me in Runcorn.

Sue had gone to spend her last night as a single woman with her parents in North Wales so it was just me, Arthur and his partner in my Runcorn house. We got stuck into eating the lovely meal previously prepared by Sue and as the drinks flowed Arthur started asking some uncomfortable questions as to why I had not invited more of our family to the wedding; something that had obviously been preying on his mind.

The mood deteriorated into heated arguments and I pointed out to him that I had not expected him to incur so much expense, but Sue had wanted to meet him and was looking forward to seeing them both. The atmosphere had turned sour and my first meeting with Arthur's partner was one I did not wish to repeat. I pointed out to the two of them that if they had any issues over the fact that I didn't invite anybody else they should have voiced them long before my wedding day!

The next morning, rather than anticipation, I felt very tired and unhappy due to the way they had both had a go at me which I felt was unfair and unjust. On the morning of the wedding I had arranged to meet the guests in a lovely pub near the church but I was still upset, had hardly slept and so drank rather heavily. It was only a short walk over to the church and inside we all took our places within its beautiful interior. The church was best known because of its connection with Lewis Carroll who was famous for writing children's novels and nonsense verse. An artist named Geoffrey Webb designed a stained glass window for the church which shows a nativity scene attended by both Carroll and Alice (in Wonderland) and panels featuring many of the author's famous characters (White Rabbit, the Dodo, Knave and Queen of Hearts, and of course, The Cheshire Cat).

When Sue eventually walked down the aisle with her father, she looked beautiful in her wedding dress and I couldn't have asked for a better bride. I had to pretend that everything was okay with me and my brother and his girlfriend so I put on a brave face and put my family tensions to one side. I stood at the altar with my future wife and focussed on what really mattered: the ceremony and our wedding vows.

It was a cold December day; fine snowflakes began to fall. Upon arrival, we were greeted by our host with glasses of champagne which we enjoyed amidst the magnificent décor. Up until 1998, Crewe Hall was still part of the property of the Duchy of Lancaster and belonged to the Crown. The décor was magnificent; we really did feel like royalty as we headed for the reception with its monumental marble fireplace and surrounding heraldic lions

Crewe Hall, Cheshire's 17th Century Mansion and Grade 1 listed hotel surrounded by beautifully landscaped garden.

We then filed into the dining room that really was 'fit for a queen'. When the time came time for Brian's speech he joked that he was happy to give his daughter away for a £5 dowry. I 'accepted' and asked him whether he needed a receipt. He never replied so this joke remains with us all to this day and I assume that he was very happy with the sale!

CHAPTER SEVEN

THE BIG FAMILY FALLOUT

Sue's mum and dad had always wanted to retire and live abroad somewhere in sunny climes. I'm not sure who came up with the idea, but it was suggested that we could immigrate to France to own and run a B&B business. Sue's parents would finance the biggest share of the business and property, then we would run the business and all live in the same house. The idea gradually grew on us as it would help to solve some of our financial problems, but would also give us a better standard of living in a better climate.

Our first challenge was to learn French. I was tasked (no surprise there) with sourcing a French teacher who would provide private, weekly lessons. Being severely dyslexic, it wasn't easy, but I was determined to give it my best shot. Eventually we put our Runcorn house up for sale and soon found a buyer. We paid off our remaining debts and the substantial mortgage leaving us debt-free and with a bit less to worry about. Obviously, we then had to find somewhere to live. Sue's parents owned the little cottage in Trefnant, Wales, just across from their back yard. They let us rent it at a reduced fee because all four of us were intending to move to France. It was a lovely property and we were really happy as Sue liked to be near her parents. I was able to get some work with Sue's brother Tom (not his real name) who was renovating a club in Chester so I was commuting each day to work on the club then back in the evening. This arrangement provided me with some work and funds until the time came for us to move and familiarise ourselves with the different lifestyle and culture. After doing some research and reconnaissance which involved many shorts trips to various parts of France, we searched for the ideal location to live. A year later we narrowed our search down and found ourselves staying in a small village just a few miles west of Montpellier in the southern Occitanic region.

Brian and Pauline had a room in a beautiful property next to where we were staying, so in the mornings we would emerge and walk the short distance to where her parents were staying. Then her mum would cook breakfast for us all. One day, Brian got up early and asked me whether I would like to go with him to the local bakery. Unfortunately, his way of 'asking' involved shouting up at our window, loudly and quite offensively. This wasn't the first time that he had spoken to me so peremptorily, but I had always kept quiet because I didn't want to put a spanner in the works and cause unnecessary tension with Brian and Pauline who were rested retirees. He seemed to have forgotten that this trip to France was meant to be a short holiday for Sue and myself because we had been working long hours over an extended period back home. So not only had Brian woken us up, but he had also insulted us by whatever he felt like saying at any time or place without thinking of other people's feelings. However, this apparently inconsequential incident was probably a blessing in disguise, because it made me realise that was how it would be if and when we lived together in France. He went to the bakery alone and I later had a 'chat' with him, stating my annoyance at his manner and that I wouldn't be joining them for any meals or activities while we were away on this so-called 'holiday'. This put Sue and her mum in an awkward position. After returning home, our friendship deteriorated so much that there was no more dialogue or meetings, so obviously the writing was on the wall. The move to France for a new life together would not be happening. It was dead in the water.

It was around November 2008 and Sue and I now had to take stock and re-evaluate our life. We knew that we could not stay in the cottage any longer because the atmosphere was strained and we were only paying a reduced rent. Sue had been made redundant from her job with a financial company so both of us were living out of suitcases, unemployed and homeless. We did have some savings left after the sale of the house in Runcorn. So I suggested to Sue that we could put all our furniture and belongings in storage, and travel around New Zealand then Australia. She was initially a bit reluctant because of the wrench from her family, but came around to the idea. We didn't make any plans for our three-week tour of New Zealand, but we did agree to visit my brother Arthur then possibly tour the North Island. We arrived in Auckland and we were tired and jet-lagged. After breakfast in the city centre hotel, we noticed that organised package tours were being offered at reception. The agent suggested that a three-week motorhome hire would save us money on hotels and car-hire. This seemed a good idea and the best option we then signed -up for the hire of the motorhome for about three weeks. We collected our six-berth vehicle and stocked up with food, and plenty of alcohol. After crossing Auckland Harbour Bridge, the second longest in New Zealand, we headed north not having a clue or caring where we were going. We were carefree on our adventure of a lifetime. It was prohibited to make overnight stops in laybys so we continued north until we found a campsite only a few yards from the beach. The campers were very welcoming, we could access a power supply and the onsite facilities meant we did not need to do any cooking on board this was a great start for us.

Our first night camping on the east coast of the North Island.

We toured the North Island stopping at different campsites, which were reasonably priced, well organised and situated near towns and coastal areas. I was keen to-visit Wellington and the southern end of the North Island where I had gone after I missed the ship in Auckland and was sent to prison. I wanted to re-visit the bar where the police picked me up. Many years had passed since those eventful times but walking through the town brought back memories of my youth and the 'good life'. The weather was glorious and bright and seemed to be smiling on our trip. The time had come for us to head up the west coast to New Plymouth and meet up with Arthur and his family.

View of Mount Taranaki showing Fanthams Peak on the southern flank

We met him over a beer in the harbour of New Plymouth then went home to meet his South Korean girlfriend Sally (he'd ditched the other one), his daughter Claudine and her son Charlie then later we met Robina, Arthur's eldest daughter, and her family. Arthur had obviously done well for himself with his swimming pool, tennis court and immaculate garden. We had 'the tour' then adjourned to the pub. After spending a few fantastic days with Arthur and his family we headed off with still about a week until we had to return the van. Arthur had recommended we see Rotorua, and that we would enjoy the hot springs and the town, so we drove over to the east side of the island to spend a few days there before driving north, back to where we started from Auckland.

Rotorua-geyser region - North Island

Rotorua - North Island, N.Z. It is one of the geothermal parks in the Rotorua region. Geysers, hot mud pools and steaming craters can be seen in this magnificent location

Time was running out for our fantastic holiday in New Zealand, and it had left us in no doubt what a wonderful country it was. We returned the campervan in Auckland and boarded our four-hour flight to Sydney. New Year was fast approaching so we were anticipating the celebrations in Sydney Harbour.

Warm-up to the New Year celebrations

The best view was down by the harbour so on the day we got up early and headed for the dock area. We had walked to the nearby Royal Botanic Gardens where to our amazement, we saw hundreds of grey-headed bats flying around and hanging from the trees. We didn't expect to see this but it was a great experience watching these creatures extending their wings whilst clinging onto the branches. We found a perfect viewing spot at the front of the Opera House, and around midnight all hell broke loose as the harbour bridge came alive. Cacophonous screeching, fizzing and banging made us hold our ears. Small boats bobbed around laden with pyrotechnics of mind-boggling diversity and ear-popping bangs and fizzes. The crowds were gasping at the silhouettes illuminating the dark sky and screams could be heard from the excited children.

Seeing this spectacle 'live' rather than televised was a mind-blowingly powerful introduction to Sydney. We planned to spend a week in Australia before heading home. I wanted to visit the pub once known as Monty's Bar in Piermont near Sydney Harbour Bridge.

I thought to myself, would it be the same? How would I feel after all these years returning back to our pick-up joint?

Walking through the doors brought my Navy memories flooding back when this was our local watering hole. Monty's was known to seafarers throughout the world.

I made my way towards the dim-lit bar.

'G'day yeh wanna coldie?' said the barman.

'Bet yeh one of those Pommy sailors who revisit this place to reminisce about the good old days with our Sheilas? I reckon.'

'Yes, I would like a cold one, and yes I'm here to reminisce.'

Just sitting at the bar sipping a cold beer and looking around the weathered walls I could still see the holes where lifebuoys and other artefacts once hung on the parapets. The barman told me that he had heard many stories of what used to go on from salty, nostalgic old sea-dogs come to revisit their old haunts. It certainly brought it all back, happy days.

To make the most of our dwindling time, we booked a hotel in Brisbane not far from the Gold Coast which only entailed a short flight. Our balcony faced the beach and the azure waters of the Pacific Ocean. We visited the late Steve Irwin's Zoo in Queensland near the Sunshine Coast. A bus ride away, it was absolutely amazing, although its vastness – it covered 1,000-acres – made it impossible to get around in one day. The crocodile pool was a highlight with Irwin's widow, Terri, teasing the reptiles with their dead rat lunch snacks. Daughter Bindi (a chip off the old block) provided the running commentary.

Steve's wife Terri

The next morning, we packed for the long flight to Los Angeles with a night stopover, then the final leg of the journey back to Manchester via London. Our hotel in LA was a jaw-dropping $250 per night and that was *exclusive* of meals. This was unacceptable, so we trekked down the endless sweep of the *Main Street* towing our luggage, tired and annoyed, until we found another hotel. It was tiresome as we needed to rest for the early flight home the next day. During the night, I could hear Sue coughing and restless. Neither of us slept well and woke up with only three hours before our flight! Sue looked pale and peaky, leaving me concerned if she was fit to fly.

A postponed flight would entail the expense of rebooking and additional hotel costs. Our only option was to rush to the airport and hope for the best but Sue was finding it heavy going especially the lengthy security and customs procedures. Sue's condition was becoming very concerning and I urged her to rest. I swapped seats with an understanding passenger who had a whole row to herself to make my wife more comfortable and she managed to sleep all the way back to London. There followed an interminable eight hour wait for the connecting flight to Manchester. I managed to get some medication from a pharmacy to tide Sue over while she rested on some empty seats. Both of us were trying to get some sleep and as a result I suddenly heard our names rasping through the tannoy, then 'final call' for our flight to Manchester. I couldn't believe my ears. In total panic I ran back to Sue and shook her. She looked really ill and I was worried. We hurried along to the gate with me clinging onto two big suitcases,—sweating and both absolutely worn out. We were embarrassingly informed that the flight had been delayed due to us being late.

On board, we were subjected to hostile stares from inconvenienced passengers who obviously blamed us for the delay. Luckily, Sue had booked us into a Manchester B&B for a few days upon our arrival home as we were still technically 'homeless'. Once in the taxi, with a very poorly wife at my side, I stared out into the dark and lashing rain and couldn't help comparing the horrible contrast with this and the past few sun-drenched and happy weeks. The situation felt like a bad 'B' movie. I could see through fogged windows that we were driving down some back lanes that eventually led to a farm. When I opened the cab door there was nothing but a sea of mud. A woman then appeared from behind a broken-down tractor and an unpleasant-looking dog leapt towards us and the grey-haired, weather-beaten woman trudged through the mud behind it. This was more than enough for me. I told Sue we were 'out of there' as it was in the middle of nowhere and we would not be able to get to the shops for food or anything else. Before the woman had a chance to speak to us I told the cab driver to turn around and take us back to the airport so we could book into a hotel. We ended up spending five days in that hotel until Sue had a chance to recover from her ordeal. The perfect end to a perfect trip!

CHAPTER EIGHT

WE ARE ALL EQUAL

In January 2009, we moved to South Manchester. This area offered a lot of potential for employment plus easy access to the motorways and nearby Altrincham and Sale. After our extensive travelling we had to set up home and live as frugally as possible. Before we had left the airport hotel we found a rented flat - a two bedroomed, Victorian property in Sale, Cheshire. The rent was high but there was plenty of room and off-road parking. We shared a cheap, second-hand car that I bought locally. Sue soon found work in a local care home, which was hard work with long hours but she enjoyed it. I struggled to find work, so we paid the rent and bills out of the remainder of our savings. I needed to keep active so I joined the local gym in Altrincham and bought a bicycle so I could get around when Sue needed the car. I eventually managed to get a job delivering medication and prescriptions for Boots. Being new, I was given the most difficult, time-consuming deliveries whilst 'the favourites' got the cushy jobs. As the medication was vital, there was a lot of pressure, so I didn't enjoy the job. I also encountered the usual backstabbing. But on a positive note, the job was part-time so I acted on a longstanding interest in photography and enrolled on a course at Manchester College. Although mainly practical, the course involved an element of written assignments and it was soon noticed by my peers that I was struggling with grammar and spelling. I was encouraged to take some assessment tests which, out of embarrassment, I was initially very reluctant to do. I eventually took the tests and as suspected, not only was I dyslexic, but it was diagnosed as 'severe'. The college provided a study coach, a laptop and assistive software, which was hugely helpful in improving my skills and after two years, I successfully achieved my foundation degree.

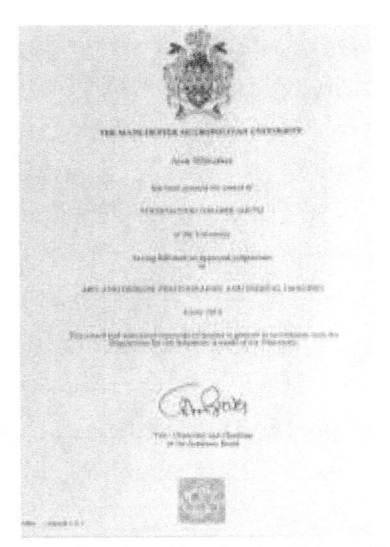

Foundation Degree from The Manchester Metropolitan University

My real interest, however, was in developing my photography techniques. I visited venues such as the Velodrome near the Etihad Stadium in Manchester, Chester Racecourse on Ladies' Day and most memorably Ricky Hatton's boxing academy in Hyde to photograph his clients in training; I even got a chance to enter the ring while Ricky was sparring. My biggest opportunity came when I contacted the marketing and media office at the Trafford Centre, Manchester. I could not believe my luck when they asked me if I would like to photograph their fashion day event which was being hosted by the television presenter and fashion expert Gok Wan. I would provide them with some images from my shoot for their website and a small fee would be paid to me for my contribution to their marketing department (an offer I couldn't refuse).

On the day of the shoot, I was nervous but excited at the prospect of shooting a live event with Gok and his models. The show was held in the vast Orient Food Hall where there was a huge walkway for the models to show their outfits. My all-access pass gave me the freedom to roam at will. I was channelling Bailey and Rankin as I ducked and dived with my cameras swinging on my shoulder. The atmosphere was electrifying as the crowds began to weave their way from the kitschy taverns, and the faux Chinese and Thai temples for which the centre is renowned. The space was designed to look like a steam ship (in homage to the nearby Ship Canal) which I had sailed up and down in so many times with its bridge and wheelhouse towering over the catwalk. 'Egyptian' statues incongruously encircled the ship as the models paraded their outfits that brought the setting to life with their glittering costumes. They looked as though they were auditioning for a part in the TV series *Downton Abbey* as some modelled their glamorous 1920s evening gowns and others their sportier casual wear.

Then came the man himself: Gok Wan. He appeared from backstage in all the glory of his glittery and colourful outfits which were a riot of mismatched maroon and cerise that perfectly complemented the design chaos of their surroundings.

By the end of the evening I had achieved my objective and went home with a smile on my face knowing that the shoot had gone better than I had hoped, and I was able to supply the marketing department with enough images for them to pay me for my time. They said I could return whenever there were any shows on at the Trafford Centre. At last, I had gained a degree of confidence in my improving written skills, and also in using my camera on a semi-pro level. I had learnt not to let dyslexia prevent me from achieving my goals.

In early 2012, I received a phone call from my younger brother Michael in Wythenshawe, Manchester. He told me that our sister who had been adopted had discovered where we used to live at Bowland in Baguley. I was so shocked that I couldn't answer him. I tried but I could not get the words out.

Then I managed to say, 'You're joking. Come on, you're joking, don't wind me up!'

'I'm not,' he replied.

I could not believe it and asked Michael how she had managed to track him down.

His reply was, 'Apparently, she and her two daughters found out where we lived and grew up as kids, and they knocked at the house next door.'

'My mate answered and he gave them my address.'

Our sister's adopted name is Karen although it was Christine originally. She had tracked us down by asking social services for her adoption papers. I asked Mike for her contact details but he was so shocked that for a while there was just silence on the line. He stammered her phone number and then hung up. Despite the fact that we had never met, I decided to speak with her for the first time in our lives. It felt weird, and I'm sure it was also the same for her. Despite having so much I wanted to say, I ended up saying very little and let her talk instead for a surreal twenty minutes or so. She briefly told me about her family and her adopted mother. She lived in

Stockport, Cheshire, not far at all, so we arranged to meet up on an agreed date and rendezvous in her local Stockport pub.

That night I could barely sleep, tormented by my churning thoughts. A few days later, I was receiving calls from the rest of my family as Karen had since spoken to them. At this point, it might be enlightening to let Karen speak in her own voice and tell her side of this momentous time:

Karen's own words…

I rang social services and a lady came to my house and handed me my adoption file. My adopted mum was with me and I was shocked when told that I was the youngest one out of eleven. My mum was struggling with it at first but she came around to accepting it. I wouldn't hurt her for the world.

My daughters and I went to the house where the Whittakers all lived because I could not settle without finding my long-lost family. I have never felt 'adopted' all these years because my mum has treated me just like one of her own. My two girls and I went and knocked on the house where the Whittakers lived at number 9, Bowland Road, Baguley in Wythenshawe. A woman came to the door and said she did not know anything about the Whittaker family, but when one of my girls mentioned Beverley (our youngest sister at the time who had died), she said, 'You need to knock next door. I think the people that live there were here at the time the Whittakers were living here.

We knocked next door and a guy said that he was Mike's friend (another one of my brothers). We then went to Mike's house, which wasn't too far away, and were informed that he was in the pub. My daughters returned to Mike's house a few days later. Jean (Mike's wife) said he turned white when he was told about me knocking on his door, and when he questioned the girls he was convinced that I was his sister who had been taken away for adoption at Wythenshawe Hospital.

My eldest brother David had passed away but I learnt that he had dictated a letter for me which his wife Angela wrote for him. I was very curious to know what was in this letter, so I went to see Angela. It was apparently in the attic and I think she was reluctant to give it to me. She told me that David had been to Wythenshawe Hospital just after I was born to try and see who was adopting me.

Arthur (my other elder brother) had named me Christine after his girlfriend. David had requested in his letter that Angela (his wife) was not to tell anyone about it, but it had to be given to me if I ever came looking for any of you all.

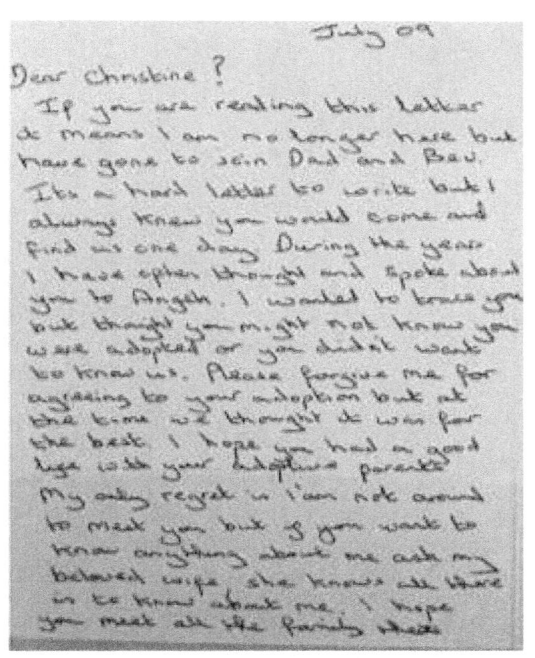

Copy of the original letter that David wrote to Karen/Christine Used with permission.

In July 2012, we arranged a family reunion. This was challenging as most of the family lived in North Wales. My mother had moved my younger brother Michael and all the girls there not long after my dad died. My mother and sisters, Susan and Carol, lived on Anglesey; sister Patricia lived in Llandudno and sister Linda lived near Rhyl.

Mike and I arranged for the event to take place at a Llandudno hotel. Even my brother Arthur came over from New Zealand and this meeting would be the first time that my mother would have seen her baby daughter after she was taken away for adoption. I guess she thought she would never see her again.

Karen and our mam in Llandudno July 2012, reunited

Karen in the orange shirt meets her sister Susan

Left: sister Carol (middle in black coat), sister Patricia with Mam (right) and friends

Brother Arthur who had travelled from New Zealand for this special day with Jenna Linda's daughter

From left to right: Arthur, Karen, Pat and my mam

A mere few months after this memorable day, my mam became very ill and was admitted to hospital in Bangor, North Wales. She had been sick for some time, but was now very ill and needed to be cared for by nursing staff. My sisters kept me updated about her deteriorating condition. My mam had been through a lot in her lifetime, raising a big family through many hardships, but she managed to live a long life with the help and support of her family and latterly, her long-lost daughter Karen. On August 13th 2013, (more 13s) she passed away peacefully surrounded by most of her loving family who kept an overnight vigil in the early hours of the morning at her bedside in hospital. She passed away the next morning, it was a very emotional time, as we said our tearful goodbyes. I phoned my brother Arthur in New Zealand to let him know – it was a difficult call to make. The only consolation we had during this awful time was that our mother had been reunited with her lost youngest daughter before she departed us all.

My Late Baptism

I was never sure if my parents were religious or not, but I remember going to Sunday service on occasions. Apart from singing hymns in school service and saying prayers, that was about all religion and faith amounted to back then.

However, I have always believed in Jesus. I have no recollection of myself or my brothers and sisters ever having been christened or baptized and can only imagine because we were too poor. It would not have been appropriate to attend the church ceremonies because of the cost of the christening gowns and clothes. I had always felt as though I had lost out having missed this wonderful occasion. Whilst considering this important step, I visited the impressive, 1855 grade II listed church of St Margaret's in Altrincham, Cheshire. Its soaring hammer beam roof with carved angels, modelled on Westminster Hall in London, cannot help but give worshippers a sense of awe. I spoke to churchwardens Dr Sue Elves and Christine Armstrong who were very welcoming so I started to attend regular Sunday services. This introduced me to St Margaret's vicar, the delightful Rev. Jerry Sutton, who was very encouraging about my wish to be baptized at such an advanced age. He said he would be happy to perform the ceremony and I was finally baptized in 2012, then confirmed in 2013. From that moment, on I felt fulfilled in my belief as a Christian. I just felt 'whole' again and at peace with God.

Open University

Away from the dramatic family events and a job that was hardly fulfilling, I was keen to further develop my skills. The study skills support received whilst studying for my photography short course at Manchester College in 2012 had given me the confidence to try something else. I enrolled on an (online) Open University Creative Writing course in the same year. It was very challenging as the modular course structure meant regular written assignments, marked with formative feedback by my allocated tutor. I had to achieve over 40% to pass each module. Nevertheless, I battled through with grim determination despite the hurdles created by my dyslexia and graduated with a Bachelors of Arts degree in 2014.

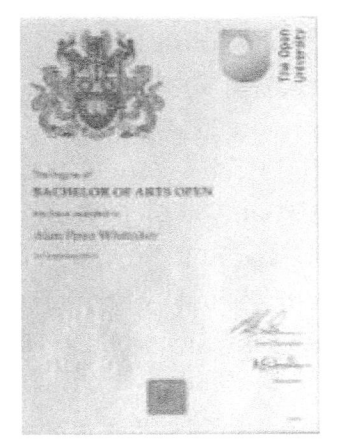

Bachelor of Arts in Creative Writing

That same year after completing the course I wanted to improve my photography and take it to a higher level so in 2014 I applied to Salford University for a place on their BA photography course. After I graduated with a BA (Hons) in photography sometime later, I was in a position where I wanted to take my writing beyond my earlier BA with the Open University. Although my successes were already beyond my wildest dreams, I still wanted to improve my writing until

I could be confident enough to write articles with my own accompanying photographs.

BA (Hons) Photography

Now that I had a foot in the door of Salford University, I contacted the senior lecturer in creative writing, Ursula Hurley. She invited me to an interview where we discussed my goals regarding creative writing. She was pleasant, intelligent and very easy to converse with. At the end of our discussion, she invited me onto the course, which delighted me. Looking back to my first academic success at Manchester Metropolitan, I would never have imagined that I could achieve so much after little formal education and struggling with dyslexia.

However, the first module was extremely challenging. The pass mark for a Master's degree was higher being 50 percent rather than the hitherto 40 percent. To my dismay, I failed the first unit. I was reassured by my lecturer that the first module was split into two units so I was still in with a chance. I scored a higher mark in aggregate so my overall marks were just above the pass required. I had ongoing guidance from Ursula and Scott Thurston who was also very helpful in reassuring me that I would succeed.

I had learnt to value the tremendous input from study skills tutors and staff trained in disability support. Whilst on the creative writing Master's course I met my new study coach, Anne Fernie, a very bright and cheerful soul. After an initial chat we seemed to get along really well, then after looking at some of my writing, she pointed out to me what areas needed to be developed. She had a wealth of knowledge about various helpful websites along with strategies that helped me to research using software and to overcome study problems thrown up by my dyslexia. She undoubtedly helped me to improve, not only writing and grammar, but also boosted my confidence as a severe dyslexic. Anne (and colleagues like her), are very experienced in helping people like myself who may be struggling with their studies. I was very lucky to have Anne as my study coach. She was, and is, a great asset to the university and her students. I have nothing but admiration for this wonderful person to whom I will be dedicating this book.

From then onwards I seemed to improve. Now that I had passed the first hurdle, I started to enjoy the course. I did make it to the finishing line and graduated with a merit, which is a good grade and one to be proud of.

Graduation day at Salford Quays
Scott Thurston and myself

My Master's Degree in
Creative Writing and Innovation

I thought I would try my hand at submitting writing for public consumption. In July 2016, I wrote an article, 'Salford University Graduate Cuts: Anguish for Students with Disabilities' for the *Salford Star* online news site about my experiences as a severely dyslexic, mature student. It was motivated by looming Tory cuts to support for disabled students, which would severely impact their applying for further education and their wider career prospects. During the course in 2017, I got the chance to put more of my newfound journalistic skills and photojournalism into practice. I had noticed the disgusting amount of fly tipping in what used to be the back area of my family home in Wythenshawe. I submitted an article with photographs to the local weekly newspaper the *Wythenshawe Reporter,* which was accepted. Gratifying proof of the 'power of the pen' occurred soon after, when I learnt that after the article had appeared, all the rubbish had been cleared and secure gates erected to deter any more fly-tipping.

These gates were erected and the rubbish taken away after my article was published on the local Wythenshawe Reporter. My childhood house was located at the other side of the bushes on the left-hand side.

Now that I had some formal qualifications under my belt, I felt confident enough to keep up with various writing projects as well as embarking on the autobiography you are reading now. Despite such work being very challenging, I feel it is important, as it may encourage readers who may have experienced similar obstacles and setbacks. If it can influence and encourage them to overcome their own challenges and never give up, then my job is done!

On the paid work front, things were less fulfilling. In 2015, I became fed up working for Boots. It was becoming increasingly clear that I was not being treated fairly regarding the daily runs of delivering and collecting medication. It was time to move on.

I saw a vacancy for a 'patient transport ambulance driver' with Arriva, a company more known for its bus and train service. They also had the ambulance service contract for the North West. My role was outlined at the interview in their headquarters in Oldham. It would entail attending to, transporting and caring for patients, which suited me as I like helping people. The two-hour interview was intense but I survived it and secured the job subject to a medical and an ambulance-driving test. The salary was minimum wage, a paltry £7 per hour, the same as given to poorly paid auxiliary workers. The first week involved training followed by a six-month probationary period during which I worked alongside other experienced drivers. Following this, I was signed off and able to work as a sole driver. The smart uniforms made me feel like a real professional, which was fulfilling. After I had been in the role for a couple of years. Arriva lost the contract, which reverted to the North West Ambulance Service (NWAS). With the help of Unison (who negotiated on our behalf), our terms and working conditions started to improve. This move over to the ambulance service was a leap forward from the unrewarding job at Boots. It involved taking sick people and children to and from hospitals in the North West (and sometimes even further afield) for special treatment in other clinics and hospitals. I felt as though I had reached my true potential by doing what I liked best, helping other people.

About the same time, my wife Sue was studying at the University of Manchester to move into nursing, whilst still working at a care home. This proved difficult for her but she was determined to succeed, and she did. Her first job was as a trainee nurse at Wythenshawe Hospital but it was not too long before she qualified and was then promoted to Sister. She was in her element and her peers noted how determined she was to move up the ranks.

Sue and her mum, Pauline, were very close but in 2015, Pauline developed cancer and became very ill. She didn't have long to live. She was a lovely person with whom I had a warm relationship so the whole family was devastated. Her deterioration had a big impact on Sue's wellbeing. Her mum had reached the point where she needed full-time care. Sue had to take a break from her job to care for and look after her mother whilst staying at her brother's house for the duration. Not long after, my wife phoned in the early hours of the morning, sobbing. I knew what was coming: Pauline had peacefully passed away, leaving behind a loving daughter and family.

The flat that we were renting in Sale became too much of a financial burden. Sue's dad Brian (who was now living alone after his wife Pauline's death), suggested that we could buy another empty flat in the same building. He knew that we could not afford any deposit and moving expenses, so he proposed that if he could live with us on occasions he would finance a proportion of the mortgage along with any renovation costs. After signing the relevant paperwork, we moved into our new home. It was a joy to break free of rental agreements and have a chance to get back on the property ladder. Brian continued to live with us from time to time. He also had a countryside lodge in Shropshire, where he had lived with Pauline after leaving North Wales. Eventually, Brian met a new partner so we didn't see so much of him but I know that Sue was happy for him after such a sad loss.

During 2018, I had often posted online comments on the The British Merchant Navy Old Friends website requesting information about the time that I sailed on the *Port Montreal* with my brother Arthur. I eventually received some exciting news from one of our old friends, Trevor Bodiam. He answered my call for old friends as he had once sailed on a ship with my brother, Arthur, with whom he had been a buddy. We swapped stories about our time on the *Montreal* and it was like a reunion with a long-lost brother. He had moved to Australia, married, and divorced, thereafter relocating to Budapest with his new partner Annamaria for a new life.

She had a second-hand shop in Budapest so they were constantly on the look-out for artefacts and antiques to sell. I suggested that it would be great if we could meet after nearly fifty years. He soon called me to say that they would be travelling to Warrington as part of a buying trip in the UK. This was only a short distance from where I live in Sale so I was ecstatic. Almost half a century since we had last met face-to-face, which seemed unbelievable.

All I could think of before our September reunion was whether he had changed and if we would recognise each other. We arranged to meet up in Altrincham. As we were both staunch Beatles fans, I suggested that I would be wearing my Beatles T-shirt in order to 'stick out like a sore thumb'. As I peered across the car park, I hoped to spot him before he saw me. I could see this middle-aged stranger heading towards me, and as he got closer he politely called out my name. I froze and couldn't reply. I suddenly recognized the smile of the young man I had known and sure enough it was Trev followed by his lovely wife Annamaria.

We shook hands, embraced and headed to a bar in Altrincham. As I looked at Trev, the sense of lost time was eerie. After catching up we returned to our flat for some grub and a few more drinks, swapping stories and agreeing to keep in touch. This was a great, albeit surreal moment in my life, but without the help of The British

Merchant Navy Old Friends website, none of it would have been possible.

Trevor and me after nearly fifty years

Now that I was working for the Northwest Ambulance Service, I began to enjoy my job much more because it is part of my nature to help people, especially the sick and vulnerable. My role with the service was known as PTS (Patient Transport Service). The global Covid-19 virus resulted in the first national 'lockdown' in March 2020. The NHS and especially A&E was placed under tremendous strain. As a consequence, I was asked if I'd like to transfer to the A&E side of the ambulance service. This involved three full days of training with the paramedics and their blue-light ambulances. I did not hesitate to volunteer and play my part in combating this virus and assisting the professionals. The training was intense. We packed so much into those three, long days to give us the experience to help and assist our colleagues in their hour of need. My role as a PES driver has given me the pleasure of working with a frontline team from all three stations in South Manchester: Sharston, Sale and Altrincham and many other crews from the North-West. Crewing up with paramedics and EMTs and the urgent care drivers has been a real experience. I have been able to witness first-hand how supportive everybody has been within the Trust. Wearing the uniform has been an honour. Seeing the level of respect and affection from the public has made me realise the important role of all the people, and fantastic NHS staff, I have had the great pleasure of working alongside and who have been at the forefront of this pandemic. In retrospect, I am glad that I took the chance to volunteer; it was an experience that will be with me for a long time to come.

Nobody expected the virus to linger so long. Like the First World War, we all thought it 'would be over by Christmas'. While it rages, people struggle to retain some normality in their lives, fret over the little things and worry whether anything will ever be normal again but joy and tragedy continue regardless of Covid-19, and my family were no different. My niece, Claire, (daughter of my younger brother Michael) passed away on Good Friday 2020. She was only forty-one, a lively and pretty girl, always fun to be with and with whom I was very close. It was like having another daughter rather than a niece. However, she had been ill for some time and was constantly in and out of Wythenshawe Hospital for various reasons. She was a very poorly girl and I felt sorry for her. My wife Sue and I visited her when she was in hospital. On occasions, we would meet up for a coffee in Altrincham but always squabbled about whose turn it was to pay for the drinks. This was a standard joke between us because when it came down to it Uncle Al was always the one to cough up (but I guess that's what uncles are for!). I will never forget the day and date, the 10th of April, 2020 that I received a call from my sister Linda sobbing her heart out.

'Hi Lin, what's up? You sound really upset.' I asked with foreboding. She just broke down and told me that Claire had died that morning on Good Friday.

The call was very short and afterwards I just lay in bed trying to take it all in. I ignored the ringing phone as I already knew the unspeakable news and was in no fit state to discuss it with any more family members. After breaking the news to my wife, I just lay there and reflected on all the precious moments Claire and I had shared. It was awful news. For the second time in recent years I dwelt on the tragedy of parents having to bury their child. One of the memories of my niece was a letter that she had written to me. She had kept her promise to send me a copy of a photograph of my mother's parents, as I had no photographs at all to remember them by.

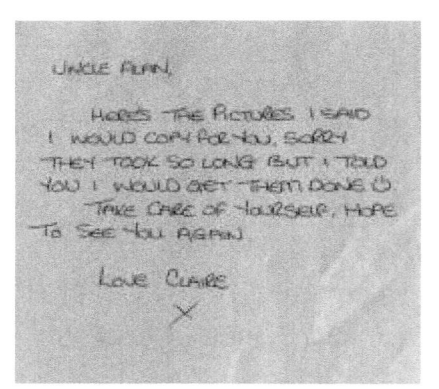

Claire's handwritten letter to me

It was very difficult bringing myself to speak with her father Mike as I knew that he adored her and that she had been a huge part of his life. What made it even more difficult was that we were in the midst of a pandemic so I was not even allowed to visit my grieving brother. Claire had such a wide range of friends and never a bad word was said about her. She was the life and soul of every situation and precious to everyone with whom she became involved. On the day of her cremation, Claire travelled slowly in a white, horse-drawn carriage from her home to the crematorium with all her family and friends walking behind. She will always be in my thoughts, such a lovely young soul; so young with so much to live for. I tend to believe that things happen for a reason, but how could such a young and carefree person be taken away from us?

Life, however, goes on.

It became apparent that I could not continue working with the worsening pain that I was getting from my right thigh and hip and I was in increasing discomfort. This started in early February 2020. However, I wasn't sure how this problem accrued, but I think over time due to my continued fitness regime I might have over done things which had brought on this unpleasant pain.

So, I was put on sick leave for a fortnight. The uneasiness continued to worsen so the GP referred me for an ultrasound scan that revealed that I had Trochanteric Bursitis, an inflammation of the 'bursa' on the outer edge of my hip. My excessive use of the gym and cycling tournaments in which I had participated over the years had no doubt exacerbated the original damage. Consequent physiotherapy sessions seemed to increase rather than alleviate the pain, so a couple of months later I had a hip X-ray to rule out any serious issues. At my subsequent appointment, the GP informed me that I 'just' had a mild form of arthritis around the hip. Once again, I was prescribed medication and more physio. Having always been very active, all this stress and emotional upheaval began to take its toll on my physiological wellbeing and just to make matters even worse I was now faced with a crisis within my marital relationship.

I had known for some time that my marriage to Sue had deteriorated and that we seemed to have drifted apart. Lately, there had been times when I had confronted her about issues in our life. I was always the one to raise them. Sue would just listen but would never respond or argue back. This always infuriated me to the point where I would shout because I became frustrated at her keeping quiet and not responding. I needed to have dialogue in order to work through our differences but always felt as though I was on my own. It started to feel as though I never had a wife with whom I could communicate and discuss my problems. Sue had many close friends and family in contrast to me.

I have always been a loner due to losing trust in people and because of this I never had any friends to confide in. It was early September when I confronted her about some payments that had inexplicably not been paid to our ex-landlord. Our obligation was to pay him a monthly maintenance charge as per our agreement when we had bought our flat. I had received a text message from the ex-landlord informing me that he had not received any payments for two months. This disturbed me so I asked my wife whether she was aware of this. She professed not to be but that she would investigate it. What I found strange about her response was that she seemed undisturbed about the seriousness of the situation. Shortly after this, I received another text informing me that he had checked back further only to discover that two more payments were missing I was furious and confronted my wife once again. She merely repeated her first response of knowing nothing but that she would resolve it. At this point, I could no longer hold back my anger and disappointment and I let her know in no uncertain terms that I had had about enough of her deceit and lies. In my distress, I blurted out that I wanted a divorce because I had had enough of her secrets and unfair attitude towards our marriage. I could not help recalling a comment made by my mother many years ago when I was a child. She averred that my father used to say that 'you know where you stand with a thief but never with a liar.' The situation worsened to the point where we were no longer on speaking terms. There was no choice but to try and live separate lives under the same roof, sharing the kitchen and lounge. The atmosphere was deeply unpleasant and tense.

About a fortnight into our silence, I was watching TV when my wife entered our living room and stated boldly that I had requested a divorce and now she was going to give me one. I had not seen this coming although it did not really catch me off guard as such. You could have cut the atmosphere with a knife as twenty years of marriage came crashing down (they say silence is golden but not in our case). Once I had regained my composure, the reality of what she had just said began to set in. I tried to explain that my outburst regarding divorce was said in anger regarding her constant lies and was not totally serious. I genuinely did not want things to go that far. It was all to no avail as she responded that she had had enough and just wanted to move on.

I did not get much sleep that night, but nothing new there. I was trying to figure out how we had let things come to such a pretty pass. My anger was also exacerbated when Sue disclosed that she had been discussing our ongoing situation with her brother Anthony prior to making her announcement to me. I thought this was wrong and disloyal. The following day she informed me that as she (and not I) had filed for divorce, costs and court fees would be charged to me. This was a heavy blow because I had no savings to pay legal costs but was left with no choice but to engage the services of a solicitor to represent me. I let a few days pass to let the heat of the situation cool somewhat, then I wrote a short letter asking her to reconsider. Her response was pleasant but unequivocal.

My letter to Sue, as I'm currently learning to touch-type this is the first time that I have typed using this method.

*This letter has not been easy for me to write, and I have given it a lot of thought before I wrote it. I know that things haven't been great between us (I've known this for some time) but whatever happens with what we are both going through with the divorce, I will always **love** you, and I am really sorry for any wrongdoing. I am* *having many sleepless nights about what the future holds. I have always loved you, even to the point where my own brother has turned his back on me (Arthur). I know that the divorce is going through and I am expecting the papers any day now. But what I'm asking you is for a little extra time to reconsider our future together. Over the last few weeks I have learnt a lot about myself, with the way I have behaved towards you.*

When I have tried to understand myself, I've realised that I have some serious sleep problems which is the cause of my state of mind. We all make mistakes and I've made my share.

It is my intention to seek some help with my sleep problems, I know I need help. I think that all the pills that I am taking for this problem are making me feel down all the time. I know that this next sentence is nothing to do with our issues, but I'm really suffering with my leg and hip pain, to a point where I can't even put my shoe and sock on. But if you were to reconsider our postponement, just for about six months, it would give us some extra time to have one last go at our marriage. And just put the divorce on hold for the time being. If you were to agree to this proposal we could just live as we are now. I will continue sleeping in the spare room. And I will do my share of the housework and other jobs. I will close now because I have said what I have wanted to say to you. We have been through a lot together and come though things before.

Thank you, Alan.

Her reply,

No Al, I respect your honesty but the petition is going ahead.

The situation critically worsened my lifelong anxiety and depression. How I yearned for a good night's sleep. It was hard to imagine what it must be like to lead a normal life, living without the fear of not being able to sleep at night. I usually wake up around 2 o' clock every morning. No matter what time I go to bed, it is always the same: lying there with crazy thoughts churning around, *did I remember to lock the front door and make my lunch for the following day's work?*

By October 2020, I knew that my marriage was over and I had tried my best. However, I was not prepared to grovel. I must admit I was shocked and was not really prepared for us to call it a day. Shortly afterwards, my wife informed me that she had purchased a new mattress for the spare room bed - no messing around there! The impending divorce also had wider financial ramifications. Our flat had come with a huge mortgage. Sue was the legal owner along with her father so both had a financial stake in the property. I had none because when we bought the flat about four years ago, I was too old to be put on the mortgage deeds. Brian, Sue's dad, had also made a considerable contribution to the renovation of the apartment which he claimed was still owed to him on the sale of the flat.

To add to my misery, my injured leg was increasingly disabling me so I began to feel less resilient and more depressed. I had continued my ambulance work throughout this period but one night, whilst working with a paramedic, we had to transfer a patient to Wythenshawe Hospital. After handing her over to the nursing staff my crewmate could see how I was struggling to cope with my leg injury. He suggested that I call our control and ask them if I could go home because I was in such pain. They agreed and I was advised to visit the GP the following day. The news however was bleak. Due to my immune system and COVID restrictions, the practice was unable to administer another steroid injection for at least another three months. It really felt as though my world had collapsed in such a short time.

Fate had not yet finished with me. It was about two months later that I decided to get out on my new bike, hoping that the exercise would ease my arthritis. It was a beautiful, sunny, life-affirming day with ideal weather conditions for a ride into the countryside. The sun beamed down and the wind was propelling me forward as though I was skippering a boat with sails. My hitherto leaden spirits soared and I felt free and happy to be able to ride this lovely, new bike. On my way home, I rode steadily observing all the rules. As an ambulance driver, I was only too aware of the potentially catastrophic outcomes when these rules were ignored. My due diligence was, however, to no avail as I negotiated a roundabout keeping flush with the left side of the road. To my horror I saw the wing mirror of a car heading at speed towards me. Before I knew what had hit me I was stunned and splayed out on the kerb surrounded by other motorists and passers-by coming to my assistance. All I recall is seeing the car when it collided with me, and my bike lying nearby. My first reaction was to grab my bike off the road to inspect any damage. On first inspection, I couldn't see any scratches or visible damage. At this point I was not sure which of the motorists had hit me from the small crowd that was gathering to offer assistance. Someone called 999 but out of embarrassment at being potentially recognised by the crew and mocked back at base, I asked him to cancel the request. The 'damage' amounted to the bicycle chain being dislodged and me with blood dripping from my hand onto the handlebars then onto the pavement. My knee was slightly cut and my wrist bruised. An elderly lady, the only bystander left by this point, admitted she was at fault for the accident. She rather uselessly gave me a tissue to wrap around my hand and kept asking whether I was alright.

 I told her I was fine because by now all I wanted to do was get my chain back on and ride home. I later discovered a broken gear-support bracket that cost about £35 to repair. Maybe I had been a bit hasty making my departure when I could have taken details and got some compensation! The more serious long-term consequence of the accident, however, was that it undoubtedly contributed to the hip replacement that was to come. The country was now on lockdown and I couldn't visit my gym. This in turn, affected my mobility and emotional wellbeing. The pain was becoming severe to the point where I was seriously considering going down the road of private medical treatment. I did not feel as though the wheels were turning quickly enough for me regarding the necessary treatment and I felt aggrieved at having to consider private medical care after 50 years of paying into the NHS and never having had a day off sick. I deserved more.

Now I not only had the worries of my forthcoming divorce to deal with and being *forced* out of my home just when I needed help the most, but also my injury. I contacted the Alexandra Private Hospital in Cheadle, Cheshire and booked an appointment with a very considerate consultant to check out my injury. I paid for the first consultation during which the Consultant Orthopaedic Surgeon suggested that I might need a total hip replacement dependent on the outcome of an MRI scan. A fortnight later, he confirmed that the hip was worn out and would need to be replaced. Although serious, this came as some relief due to the extreme pain I had been enduring.

I was dreading the potential costs of the operation, consultant fees, physiotherapy, MRI scan and medication. Luckily, the Orthopaedic Surgeon advised me that I could recoup these costs through the NHS by getting a GP's referral form. The surgeon did not usually do NHS work but recognised the extent of my physical pain, the importance of my frontline role and that with the COVID crisis ongoing, I needed to get back to work speedily. Thankfully, I got the referral and the operation was scheduled to be carried out by Mr Adam Hoad-Reddick and his team at the Alexandra Hospital Cheadle Cheshire at the end of November 2020, many months sooner than it would have been on the NHS. I have nothing but admiration for

Adam Hoad-Reddick and his PA (Lady Lucy) Lucy Forster who helped me regain my happiness and self-worth and I will always be very grateful for the help and understanding that this kind and generous man has given to me.

I write this during my period of post-surgery recovery. Building up my strength and confidence also feels like a new beginning in my life in every way. While I lay in bed sometimes I would have some unforeseen terrible thoughts of taking my own life on many occasions when I was at the lowest point of my existence. Having heard stories from my colleagues while working on the frontline in the ambulance service that there were occasions when they were called out to a patient's home, only to find that they had taken their own life. Now I found myself with the same thoughts.

Mentally I have been down some dark paths of wanting to give up and simply take my own life and be done with any further pain and misery. Why bother living like this?

Then I began to realise the true value of family and friends during this period. Because of COVID-19 I had to quarantine for two weeks. This meant that I had to be on my own, which proved very difficult considering my post-op circumstances. Luckily, my sister Linda and brother-in-law Mike, their son, Simon, daughter Jenna and her husband Dan made their house available for me to stay at for the duration of my isolation period. At this point I also want to pay tribute to my lovely daughter-in-law Nic (my son Paul's wife). She took me to the hospital on the day of my operation. Three days later, she was there for me again waiting at the hospital reception to take me to my sister Linda's house in North Wales. Both Nic and Paul have been so supportive. I love them both and want to say 'thanks' here in this book. Rachel my lovely daughter also kept in touch with me to make sure that I was okay and being looked after. My good friend 'Woodie' (Karen Wood) who I worked with on the ambulance service called at my home on many occasions to help with the shopping, which was a great help to me, thank you Woodie. This is what I would have expected Sue to do for me, in my dark days, as I would have done for her, but she didn't. I thought that she would have maybe text me to see how my operation went and how was I doing, but she didn't.

It is always best to 'look towards the light' but I do wish that Sue would have confided in me first regarding our marital issues rather than her family. So, at the age of 69, it is time to start the next phase in my adventure of a life.

I would like to retire, but due to my earlier financial circumstances with the predicament that the franchise with Captain Cargo had led me to cash-in my personal pension plan, now I only have my minimal state pension to support me now that I have had to leave the marital home.

As I bring this book to a close, I can see how my life has been a rollercoaster of ups and downs to say the least. I would like to think that the readers of this book will be able to take some hope from my story to accomplish anything that they set out to achieve, and not let any obstacles prevent them from reaching their goals.

Returning back to the important role that the Nightingale Centre played during the COVID-19 pandemic (which was originally Manchester Central Station).

From the *Manchester Evening News* 2021

This does not mean the Nightingale's role in the North-West's response to the virus is over. We must be ready for the possibility that the number of COVID-19 cases rises again as social distancing rules are eased.

Work is also underway to consider how the Nightingale's role may further adapt as the NHS seeks to resume activity that had to be paused in the first phase of our response to the pandemic.

'The hospital has been a fantastic achievement and thank you to all the organisations that supported this ambitious project, and to everyone who has worked with great energy and commitment in challenging circumstances to help save lives.

The Gurkha Rifles

A big thank you is due from a very grateful nation to the Queen's Own Gurkha Logistic Regiment (QOGLR) 60 Close Support Squadron for helping the NWAS to combat the pandemic that landed on our shores just over a year ago. It's such a great honour to be working alongside these very courageous men. They undertook driving ambulances, manual handling, kit familiarisation and basic life support before being able to work alongside professionals within the North West NHS and other trusts around the country.

These brave Gurkha soldiers from the Royal Gurkha Rifles have had a long and proud history of serving with the British Army for over 150 years. Many fought in the two World Wars and they have battled with honour and distinction in Hong Kong, Malaysia, Borneo, Cyprus, the Falklands, Kosovo, Sierra Leone, Iraq and Afghanistan. Now they are fighting an invisible war, COVID-19, alongside the NHS.

Cpl Ganesh Gurung from The Queen's Own Gurkha Logistic Regiment (QOGLR), 60 Close Support Squadron, based in Dalton Barracks, Abingdon, Oxon., writes about the regiment's experience of working with the Northwest Ambulance Service. His own words...

Working alongside NWAS whilst helping them to look after their patients is like a lifetime opportunity for us which I will remember and cherish for a lifetime and it is different to what we do normally in the army. I am enjoying my time here and learning a lot of useful skills which I am very grateful to everybody who has trained me and helped make my time here worthwhile. I am very happy that I got the opportunity to do this amazing job.

As for me I have enjoyed my short time working with the professionals and have also learnt many new skills which will benefit me for a long time to come. Whenever we see an emergency ambulance with its sirens and blue lights flashing, we can rest assured that they will be able to cope with whatever lies before them. I wrote this post for the NWAS Green-Room blog:

Back in May, PTS Care Assistant Alan Whittaker gave us his account of volunteering to work with PES crews to help in our response to COVID-19. It is now some time since the initial outbreak of COVID-19, and it became clear the level of challenges and difficulties that NWAS was up against. The transfer from PTS to PES has given me an insight into what the emergency services have to deal with on a daily basis. Since the outbreak of the pandemic there have been many difficult hurdles to be overcome.

We are now in uncertain times as to whether the virus will reappear, but one thing that I'm sure of: all the NWAS team, including the controllers, will be ready to tackle whatever comes their way. The public can be assured that they can count on people like us to give them the reassurance of receiving the highest standard of care that they expect and deserve.

Having sat in the front of an ambulance alongside the professionals, it has been impressive to see how quickly they react when the call comes through from control, they speedily swing into action. Not only have I witnessed their medical skills, but their expertise in reassuring the patients with their care and wellbeing by comforting them in these difficult times that we are all facing.

When it comes to answering that all-important call, they are quick to respond with their blue-light driving skills and sirens to alert the public that the emergency service is responding to a 999 call. My role as a PTS driver has given me the pleasure of working with the frontline teams from all three stations in South Manchester:

Sharston, Sale and Altrincham, along with other crews from the North West.

Crewing-up with paramedics, EMTs and the Urgent Care crews has been a real experience to witness first-hand how supporting everybody has been within the trust. Wearing the NWAS uniform has been an honour and gaining respect from the public has made me realise what an important role the staff have played during the COVID-19 crisis.

Looking back now to last April I'm glad that I took the chance and volunteered to help and assist our colleagues in PES. It's an experience that will be with me for a long time to come. But there's one thing that we can be sure of if we are faced with a recurrence of COVID-19: we will be more than ready to tackle whatever it throws at us.

Me working with A & E on the front-line of COVID-19

ACKNOWLEDGEMENTS

It is hoped that my story will be an inspiration to the readers of this short autobiography. I would like to thank all the people who have helped me put this story together.

First of all, my study coach, Anne Fernie, who has been a tremendous help and inspiration from the outset in providing me with confidence as a dyslexic person and guiding me through all the difficult periods of working through my grammar and spelling difficulties.

Also, a very special thank you to my lecturers from the University of Salford. Ursula Hurley, Scott Thurston, Kate Adams, Judy Kendall and David Savile. Also, to my school friend who gave me the class photo, and for the picture of the Blackburn Convalescent Home.

The neighbour that I mentioned as Mrs Peter's isn't the real name of our next-door neighbour, I have used my second name 'Peter' so as not to offend any readers who may recall our family. I have dedicated this autobiography to my beloved family.

Dad Mam
Maureen David Arthur
Linda Michael Susan
Patricia Carol Beverley
Karen who was recently united back into our family for GOOD.

REFERENCES

Dermah R. (2000). School for Seaman: The Story of the Gravesend Sea School. Buckingham: Baron Books

Dobson, C., 2021. The Nightingale North West in Manchester will close this month. [online] Manchester Evening News. Available at: <https://www.manchestereveningnews.co.uk/news/greater-manchester-news/nightingale-north-west-manchester-close-18371687> [Accessed 11 March 2021].

Encyclopaedia Britannica. 2021. Great Lakes | Names, Map, & Facts. [online] Available at: <https://www.britannica.com/place/Great-Lakes> [Accessed 11 March 2021].

Eric, P., 2021. 10 Interesting Facts About the Panama Canal - The Panama Blog. [online] The Panama Blog. Available at: <https://www.thepanamablog.com/10-interesting-facts-about-the-panama-canal/> [Accessed 11 March 2021].

Higginbotham, P. (2017). 'Children's Homes: the institutions that became home for Britain's children and young people'. Retrieved 2 January 2018 from: http://www.childrenshomes.org.uk/author/

Higginbotham, P. (2017). Children's Homes: A History of Institutional Care for Britain's Young. Barnsley: Pen and Sword
Wade, R (2013). Blackburn Convalescent Home (Thursby Home) 1916, St Annes.

HISTORY. 2021. Panama Canal. [online] Available at: <https://www.history.com/topics/landmarks/panama-canal> [Accessed 11 March 2021].

Pennmedicine.org. 2021. 1 in 4 Americans Develop Insomnia Each Year - Penn Medicine. [online] Available at: https://www.pennmedicine.org/news/news-releases/2018/june/1-in-4-americans-develop-insomnia-each-year [Accessed 11 March 2021].

Roberts a R. (1976) A Ragged Schooling: Growing up in the Classic Slum. Manchester University Press. Lancashire.
https://www.flickr.com/photos/rossendalewade upy/8649172315

Stamp, J. (2014). 'Pioneering Social Reformer Jacob Riis Revealed 'How the Other Half Lives' in America'. Smithsonian.
https://www.smithsonianmag.com/history/pioneering-social-reformer-jacob-riis-revealed-how-other-half-lives-america-180951546/ (2021)

Writer, S., 2021. What Are the Names of the Five Great Lakes? [online] Reference.com. Available at: <https://www.reference.com/geography/names-five-great-lakes-754839ee0a031a43> [Accessed 11 March 2021].

Printed in Great Britain
by Amazon